"Rabbi Edelheit guides us ¹ living in it. Through schola.......,.......... tiently explains how we Jews 'read' it. He introduces us to great biblical characters and ordinary contemporary strangers who seem to mysteriously pass through his life with their flaws, injuries, prayers, and lessons. If you're a Jew and know someone who is Christian, for the love of God, give them this book."

—Lawrence Kushner, Scholar-in-Residence, The Congregation Emanu-El, San Francisco

"In this rich and easily accessible book, Rabbi Joseph Edelheit takes a simple question—'what am I missing?'—and shows how it illuminates the lives of famous biblical characters as well as our own struggles with modern society. Despite their many virtues, Abraham, Rachel, Miriam, Moses, David, and Esther are all missing some important feature of Jewish existence. But their stories have important lessons to teach us about what it means to be human, to deal with uncertainty, to live in a pluralistic society, and to be satisfied with who we are. This is a book that needs to be read and re-read to appreciate its many valuable insights."

—Kenneth Seeskin, Professor of Philosophy and Philip M. and Ethel Klutznick Professor of Jewish Civilization, Northwestern University

"In *What Am I Missing?* Rabbi Edelheit brings new and profound insights into a wide variety of intellectual and psychological issues of the human condition. Readers of all disciplines and students of life will find hope and power in this breathtaking examination of the difficult and redemptive truths of our lives. As a professor of Jewish theology, I was moved by his examinations of biblical characters and the ways in which their struggles mirror our own and how they can mentor us in our lives today. What a treasure this book is!"

—Rabbi Rachel Sabath Beit-Halachmi, Senior Fellow, Kaplan Center for Jewish Peoplehood

"This book is a gift. Had I only had this book, I would have been far richer for it. And I can attest that what I experienced in friendship and mentorship is what is in abundance in this brilliant and crucially important book. We will all miss many great gifts in our lives, but please don't miss *What Am I Missing?*"

—Doug Pagitt, Founder and Former Pastor, Solomon's Porch, Minneapolis

"Joseph takes us on a journey interweaving important characters of Torah and his own life and the lessons we learn or don't learn by seeking out what we think we need or what society tells us we need. . . . Joe reminds us that we need to stop our fast ride through life and gather what is offered to us and to learn from it. A perfect read as we all travel through life's joys and travails and take ancient lessons into our contemporary life. A must-read for all searchers, learners, and life's active participants."

—Marilyn Price, storyteller, author, and educator

What Am I Missing?

What Am I Missing?

Questions About Being Human

Joseph A. Edelheit

FOREWORD BY

Tony Jones

WIPF *&* STOCK · Eugene, Oregon

WHAT AM I MISSING?
Questions About Being Human

Wipf & Stock
An Imprint of Wipf and Stock Publishers
199 W. 8th Ave., Suite 3
Eugene, OR 97401

www.wipfandstock.com

PAPERBACK ISBN: 978-1-7252-5902-7
HARDCOVER ISBN: 978-1-7252-5903-4
EBOOK ISBN: 978-1-7252-5904-1

Manufactured in the U.S.A.   02/13/20

To my Children

My most important life-teachers

Contents

Illustrations

Grave Marker—photo by Sinai Temple, Michigan City, IN | 8

Swastika—photo by the author—this remnant is in the Center for Holocaust and Genocide Education at St. Cloud State University, St. Cloud, MN | 37

The Star of David is from Creative Commons, Public Domain. Contributor, Tobias Schmidbauer. https://commons.wikimedia. org/wiki/File:Black_Star_of_David.svg | 65

Foreword

A rabbi and a pastor walk into a bar—it's not the start of a joke, and it actually happened in an airport lounge, but it was the start of a beautiful friendship, one that has encouraged, challenged, and sustained me for over a decade now.

Joseph Edelheit leaves an impression. He's loud and funny, with the hair of Einstein and the hug of a linebacker. He's an anomaly, a mold-breaker. He did his doctoral work in Christian theology because he wanted to better understand his neighbors. He's been the senior rabbi at prestigious synagogues and launched a religious studies department at a state college in a notoriously antisemitic town. He's stood in the Oval Office and preached from innumerable pulpits.

But none of that would matter if he couldn't do what he's done for me, and what he does in this book: open the Bible to us with care and insight. "Jews," he writes herein, "celebrate the infinite possible interpretations that link us to God's infinity." That's a lesson he's had to teach me time after time, because it is ancient wisdom that runs counter to the post-Enlightenment Protestantism in which I was reared.

In seminary, I learned that every passage in the Bible has a correct interpretation, and the harder I studied, the closer I'd get to it. My rabbi has disabused me of that notion, teaching me instead that the deeper I dig into the text, the more possibilities will open to me. Instead of foreclosing alternative readings, he's pointed me toward an infinite horizon of meaning.

In *What Am I Missing?*, Joseph follows the great rabbinic tradition of starting with a question, and an existential one at that. So many of us today wander this planet consumed with beeps and buzzes and scrolling and clicking, and it couldn't be more obvious that we're actually trying to avoid the deeper questions of meaning that all the great philosophers and hermeneuts and exegetes have been asking for millennia. And yet, as I have seen in three decades of Christian ministry, those questions come right up and slap us in the face at regular intervals, be it during a divorce or the death of a loved one or an ailment that stops us cold.

Where do we look when such episodes cause us to question our very being? The social media sites fail us at such times, as do the firehoses of breaking news on screen and in print. *Look back*, our rabbi says to us, *and commune with the patriarchs and matriarchs.*

These six brothers and sisters—Abraham, Rachel, Moses, Miriam, David, and Esther—still have much to teach us—if I may be so bold, they have infinite lessons for us.

For brothers and sisters they are, not gods nor demiurges. Each is incomplete, imperfect, missing something, just as I am, and just as you are. And here, I think, is the brilliance of Joseph's thesis in this book: these six giants of the Hebrew tradition stand in solidarity with us, for they each struggled, as we do, to know God's will, to do good, to remain faithful amidst strife. They are human! And, as Joseph writes, "Being human is about learning what is missing and living a meaningful life." For, paradoxically, we add meaning to our lives by acknowledging what is missing—indeed, that's what confirms that we are human.

I wish that each of you had the blessing of sitting with Joseph over coffee or a good meal and exploring the text with him, but that is of course impossible. However, reading this book is the next best thing. For my rabbi is a faithful and trustworthy guide into the Scripture and the lives of these six extraordinary figures. I can confirm that Joseph asks these same existential questions himself, of his own life, which makes him all the more reliable as a narrator of the human experience vis-à-vis the sacred text.

Put yourself in this rabbi's hands, as I have, and you will come to know yourself better—as well as your God.

Tony Jones
December 4, 2019
Feast of St. John Damascene
Ben-Gurion Day

Acknowledgements

I once watched as my mentor and doctoral advisor, David Tracy, perused books at the Seminary Co-Op bookstore near the University of Chicago. He would open the book at the back and read the notes and bibliography and only then look at the contents! I later asked him why and he explained that it was important to see what the author was reading in order to know if you wanted to read the book! The bibliography in this book was created with this in mind. These are among the books, essays, and articles that have informed my thinking over many years rather than just specifically items referenced in the book. My thinking is a product of many years of reading and teaching, not just writing this book.

I was invited to give the Bishop Jonas Thaliath, CMI, Lectures 2010-2011 at the Pontifical Athenaeum Dharmaram College in Bangalore, India. Though I spoke on Jewish-Christian dialogue in the twenty-first century, I used the opportunity to develop the ideas that would become this book. My host, the Reverend Father Paulachan Kachappily, graciously permitted me to keep my lectures rather than publish them so I could continue to develop my ideas.

This project has received a great deal of caring attention from its inception through its final birthing. It has been truly an experience of many good friends, and rabbinic and university colleagues. Each took the time to read and share their responses, concerns, ideas and gracious support at every single phase of my writing, editing, and re-writing of *What Am I Missing?*: Larry Rudnick, Cliff Greene, Dan Wildeson, Marla Kanengeiter, Dan Stiver, Stephanie

Arel, Jim Moore, Steve Klepetar, Paulo Geiger, Ken Seeskin, Rachel Sabath-Bet Halachmi, Sue Nadel, James Gertmenian, and Marilyn Price. Larry Kushner and Tony Jones each offered me their unconditional support and necessary "tough love" as my initial ideas became a text for which I am eternally grateful. Bill Huntzicker and Margo Kanthak shared their gifts of editing and meticulous grammar. Margo's technical talents were vital in bringing the final manuscript into formatted existence, God bless you!

One person read every single draft and then spoke honestly with concern about its tone, length, and ideas. That person was Ilana Kaufman Spector who opened her heart and life to me and transformed how I live, all of which made this book possible.

1

The Missing Piece

It has happened to everyone. You are standing at the open door looking for your keys, holding a backpack or briefcase or purse, a coffee mug, and you stop. You need to leave, the day is full, and your mind is filled with the anticipation of the next several hours, but you seem frozen by a single simple question: "What am I missing?" You race through a list, looking at everything you are holding. You try to put something down to find your phone, your wallet, your passport, your computer, and having checked mentally and physically, you are now sure. You close the door and begin your trek to the outside, but there remains a still quiet nagging question, "What am I missing?"

You are pushing the cart through a store, checking the list(s), the notes on the phone, even calling someone to double check. You do not want to get distracted, but just as you were about to finish this aisle, you spot a friend or acquaintance and pause to make some friendly conversation. You get to the checkout line muttering to yourself: "What am I missing?" As you leave the store and are putting the bags into the car, you are still sure that you are missing something.

We often relive this scene in many ways because we live busy, complex, and difficult lives that seem to be getting busier, more complex, and more difficult every day. We keep trying to make sure that we have everything we need, that we are ready for anything, and that we can finish with all of the distractions and finally do what we really want. In the process, we are continually haunted by the question: "What am I missing?"

As if our nagging self-awareness were not enough, this same question has also become a popular response of individual disbelief. When everyone else seems to understand the positive reviews of a movie, book, or person, and you can only shake your head in lone and uncertain disagreement: "What am I missing?" You understand that the majority feels one way, but the best you can do is ask, "Really?" With an unrelenting flow of opinions and reviews about everything, we are being forced to accept or reject ideas without really completing a process of thoughtfulness. Yet, whether on social media, in emails, or during office chatter, our opinion is required before we are finished, and in the face of yet another majority point of view, when in doubt, we mutter, "What am I missing?"

This book is an opportunity to take the simplicity of "What am I missing?" very seriously. We should make the effort to use this question with more awareness of its profound purpose. This question is much more than a nagging reminder of our complex needs or a quick rhetorical tool about the opinions others have or want from you. "What am I missing?" is a fascinating means of opening vital conversations about the very nature of being human. What am I missing? Asking just this simple question provides us with an opportunity to listen, reflect, and then ask another question in order to sustain the conversation.

We begin this conversation by asking ourselves, "What am I missing?" at the deepest level of our consciousness. We live in a time defined by information and data, yet most of us are missing a sense of meaning and purpose in our lives. Many of us, even those who have jobs, careers, families, and friends, are still seeking *more*. For many the search can initially be fulfilled with the "things" that we use to define our happiness or success. Our time is spent conscientiously checking our lists to certify we have found what we have always wanted: homes, cars, partners, children, then more—bigger homes, better cars, new partners.

We look to outside sources—like bosses, friends, community authorities, celebrities, and even religious leaders—to confirm that we have found what we thought we were missing. Eventually, we may realize that we have been listening to the wrong authorities. We finally take the time to review our lists and ask again with a new perspective, "What am I missing?"

We need the wisdom that can only be gained through failure that leads to real growth. Failure means we have taken risks, attempted something beyond our previous achievements. The risks lead to a different perspective, and hopefully a changed method, and then the courage to take another risk. T. S. Eliot, poet and Nobel Laurate, taught: "Only those who risk going too far can possibly find out how far one can go."[1]

The wisdom of failure guides us to begin to realize that we are missing deeper meaning, that we are getting hope not happiness, resilience not winning, purpose not prestige, and the calm that sustains a critical perspective. This list is certainly not exhaustive, just a few categories to stimulate our momentum. I have never met anyone who has it *all!*

I know some truly brilliant people, some fabulously talented people, and others who by the chance of family or business acumen are very wealthy. I have not ever known anyone whose family dynamics, social skillset, personal appearance, and friendships all converge into an always perfect, complete life. Each of us is missing both superficial and deeper elements of being whole.

Our understanding of perfect—which is highly polished and manipulated by media and advertising—is an unreachable goal. We are more than what we see in a mirror or how we happen to feel today. The industry of self-help exists because of the long list of human needs we continue to seek and still cannot find. But knowledge is never as deep nor meaningful as wisdom, which is gained only by the actually lived path of our lives.

Our bodies require so much of our attention: clothes, food, lotions, exercises, diets, massages, and an infinite number of photos. Yet, regardless of how much time, effort, and cost, most of us are still searching for "another" body: younger, taller, shorter, thinner, with more or less hair, of a different color! When we

1. Eliot, "Preface," ix.

demand of ourselves, "What am I missing?" there is always an urgency, but rarely can we accept the obvious answer even as we look in the mirror. When our search is for purpose, hope, resilience, or values, we must first demand of ourselves the honesty we experience in the mirror of reality.

In Shel Silverstein's classic story, *The Missing Piece*, the poet and illustrator has given popular culture the story of a circle with a missing piece who spends his time searching for it. When he finds it, he also learns the greater truth about himself and his search— that his identity is, in part, defined by what is missing. We too must reckon with this possibility. After acknowledging that we are missing something and being determined to find it, we might finally come to understand that we are best defined by how we live, not by what is missing. Maybe, the search was about finding a truth about ourselves and not the missing piece.

Lawrence Kushner, a writer, mystic, rabbi, and good friend, once wrote:

> There must have been a time when you entered a room and met someone and after a while you understood that unknown to either of you there was a reason you had met. You had changed the other or he had changed you. By word or deed or just by your presence the errand had been completed. Then perhaps you were a little bewildered or humbled and grateful. And it was over.
>
> Each life is the pieces of a jigsaw puzzle. For some there are more pieces. For others, the puzzle is more difficult to assemble. Some seem to be born with a nearly completed puzzle. And so, it goes. Souls going this way and that trying to assemble the myriad parts. But know this. No one has within themselves all the pieces of their puzzle. Like before the day when they used to seal jigsaw puzzles in cellophane. Ensuring that all the pieces were there. Everyone carries with them at least one and probably many pieces to someone else's puzzle. Sometimes they know it. Sometimes they don't. And when you present your piece which is worth less to you, to another,

whether you know it or not, whether they know it or not,
you are a messenger from the Most-High.[2]

When we ask, "What am I missing?" we are initiating an important self-critical awareness, that our life has at least one missing puzzle piece. When we actually experience the reality, the lived knowledge, that our life is incomplete, that we cannot finish the puzzle because we do not have all the pieces, we become open to new possibilities and growth. Critically reviewing our lives helps us recognize that we also have puzzle-life pieces that belong to others, which we alone must provide through relationships. When we unexpectedly encounter others and permit them to engage, we open ourselves to accept our needed pieces. In turn, we become open to be the source of their missing pieces, and then we too can be messengers from the Most-High.

Many years ago, I received a transformative piece of life's puzzle in an exchange from an anonymous source. What happened was absolutely real but even today beyond any explanation. During my tenure at Sinai Temple in Michigan City, Indiana, the congregation applied to the Memorial Scroll Trust. This unique institution in the global Jewish community took care of the Torah scrolls that had survived the Holocaust and offered them on permanent loan to synagogues throughout the world. After all the Jews had been exterminated, the Nazis had planned to build a museum from the sacred treasures stolen from Europe's Jews.

When Prague was liberated, a warehouse with nearly 1,600 Torah scrolls was found. Each Torah was tagged and numbered, which corresponded to the Nazi inventory lists linking the scrolls to communities and synagogues. Many of the scrolls came from communities now *judenrein*—Jew-free—where the synagogues had been destroyed. Sinai Temple received scroll #23592 (the Nazi inventory number) from Ivanczech, Bohemia.

We dedicated the Torah on Yom Kippur 1982, and the newspaper had a photo and article about the scroll and its history. Several days later, a man came to see me at the synagogue. He was thin, wore

2. Kushner, *Honey from the Rock*, 69–70.

jeans, t-shirt, and baseball cap. I welcomed him into my study, and thinking he had read the article, I asked if he wanted to see the Torah scroll. No, he said, he just wanted to thank me. The article helped him realize that he had been saving "these" for me, and then he gave me the paper bag he was carrying. He explained that he had been a nineteen-year-old infantry man who liberated Dachau concentration camp. I again offered to take him into the sanctuary and show him the Torah scroll. He shook his head, thanked me, and quickly left the synagogue. He never gave me his name.

I was left holding a paper bag, totally confused, surprised that he had left. I went looking for him, but he had walked out the front door and was gone. I sat down at my desk and opened the simple brown paper bag and found several black and white photographs, two cloth numbers with strings, and an old small bottle. I quietly picked up the bottle to look more closely; it was the old orange/brown glass and I could not be sure of its contents. I opened the top and saw quite clearly ashes and charred bones. I was stunned. I was holding remains from Dachau concentration camp at my desk at Sinai Temple, Michigan City, Indiana, in 1982.

As a Jew born in 1946, the events of 1939–1945 are essential to my life but I never actually experienced these events. As a young rabbi who felt called to serve the American Jewish community of the 1970s, the Holocaust was just beginning to be a significant role in our identity. I had taught about the Holocaust at a Lutheran university, Valparaiso, and had participated in some Jewish-Christian dialogues about post-Holocaust theology.

Nothing in any of my education or experience prepared me to be holding this bottle. I cried and tried as best I could to understand what had just happened. How was it possible that the actual reality of the six million had been brought to my office? The Holocaust is often beyond our ability to imagine, the systematic extermination of humans—men, women, and children—cannot be compared to any other state-organized and commanded slaughter. I knew and taught many facts about the extermination of my people, but this personal reference point was unexpected and remains even today a dark unexplained mystery.

My tears of disbelief were transformative. The radical evil of Europe had somehow been confirmed in my synagogue. I called the rabbi in Chicago with whom I had worked before coming to Sinai Temple. He had been a refugee rabbinic student from Germany and his father had been interned in Dachau. He was gravely silent over the phone and guided me toward my conclusions. I would bury the remains in our synagogue's cemetery in a private service. I would not make this a public event in which the "shock" would eclipse the solemn reality of our responsibility.

An anonymous man who read a newspaper article brought me things that he had kept since April 29, 1945. In the days that followed, I spoke with only a handful of people and we agreed where I would bury the remains in the Temple's cemetery in a private funeral. My secretary's husband had been in one of the US Army units that had liberated a camp, so he dug the small hole. A dear family friend had survived *Terezin/Theresienstadt* and I asked her to read some prayers. I explained to our leadership why I thought the service should be private, but that we would have a memorial stone set over the grave and invite the community.

I used the *Taliit*—prayer shawl—that I had worn on my Bar Mitzvah when I was thirteen years old to wrap up the remains of the nameless, ageless, genderless victim(s). I buried this sacred puzzle piece in a plot on a small mound at the very entrance of the cemetery. Whenever I return to Michigan City, I always go and leave a small stone on the grave marker. There is a Jewish custom of leaving a rock on a tombstone rather than flowers. Jewish law argues that one should not "mock the dead," and leaving a flower, which cannot be seen or appreciated by the dead, is considered mocking. While a simple pebble will not wither and die and is naturally egalitarian, its statement is profound—I was here with you.

1939　　זכור　　1945

THE REMAINS OF UNKNOWN

JEWISH HOLOCAUST VICTIM OF DACHAU

BURIED

OCT. 17, 1982　30 TISHRI 5743

My small stone is my way of acknowledging that God must have sent the man into my life as a Messenger from on High. Kushner's image of missing puzzle pieces has always been perfectly and mystically resonant. A man, who at nineteen brought home "souvenirs" from a Nazi concentration camp, somehow knew he had been saving them for *me*, Joseph Edelheit, a rabbi in the small town sixty-three miles outside of Chicago so that I would provide those remains a final sacred burial in a Jewish cemetery.

When telling this story, I usually acknowledge that if this is the only thing I had ever done as a rabbi, it would surely have been enough. I did not know that I was missing a piece of my purpose that could be filled by this absolutely inexplicable event. The simple and sometimes nagging question, "What am I missing?" is a means of asking ourselves much more than what I should remember at the store. Our lives are still incomplete puzzles for which we are searching for pieces. These missing pieces require that we demand of ourselves both honesty and trust. We must also be ready for the most unexpected experience of finding a piece of ourselves in a relationship with someone else.

2

Six Characters in Search of Wisdom

A wonderful story has been attributed to Rabbi Nachman of Bratslav (Breslov), one of the greatest of the Eastern European Hassidic Jewish leaders of the late eighteenth and early nineteenth centuries.

> A Jewish villager once dreamed about a treasure. In his dream the treasure was near a bridge in the city of Vienna. The very next morning, the villager packed his knapsack with his religious articles, some clothes, and a bit of food. Then he began the long, long walk to Vienna. For many days and nights, he trudged through forests and fields, valleys, and towns. When he arrived at last, the soldiers who guarded the city wouldn't let him near the bridge. So, day after day, he stood by the side of the road, trying to think of what to do. One afternoon, a soldier walked up to him and asked, "Why are you standing here?" The villager was silent for a moment. Perhaps we could be partners, he thought. After all, half a treasure is better than none! So, he told the soldier about his dream.
>
> "Only a Jew cares about dreams!" he laughed. "For three nights in a row, I dreamed that in a certain village there was a certain Jew—and he named the man's village and his name—who had a treasure buried in his cellar. But do you think I believe in such foolish things?"
>
> The villager simply thanked the soldier and began the long journey home. For many days and nights, he

trudged through forests and fields, valleys, and towns. Finally, he came to his own little house. Without even sitting down for a cup of hot tea, the man went down to his cellar and started digging. Sure enough, he uncovered a huge treasure. He was able to live comfortably and do many good deeds for the rest of his days.

Later, when people asked him about his long journey, he said, "I really had the treasure all along. But to find it, I had to go to Vienna!" *The treasure we are searching for is inside of ourselves.*[1]

We need guides in our search for both the missing pieces of our lives and our inner treasure. We all need resources that inspire, sustain, and even provoke us during this journey. Rabbi Nachman's story was meant for Jews but its message is universal. Although there are many sources of wisdom, the sources to which we turn in this book are the timeless ideas of Scripture as well as those who teach and interpret its wisdom.

And so, in our search for a greater understanding of being human, we begin with the text that is one of the cornerstones of Western culture: the Bible. It was the first book printed in 1454 on Gutenberg's press. Most scholars agree that the King James Version—the official English translation of 1611—has profoundly influenced the English language in both spoken and written form. Statistically, no other text has been read, printed, distributed, or translated as much as the Bible.

The Bible is the primary sacred narrative of both Judaism and Christianity and informs the foundation of Islam. This shared monotheistic Scripture is the source for universal and pluralistic values as well as particularistic observances. The Bible's texts have "surplus meaning"—they can be interpreted in multiple ways—and as classic religious texts are accepted as both divinely revealed and as redacted and codified over centuries. Some Christians hold biblical texts to be inerrant, while most Jews celebrate the infinite possible interpretations that link us to God's infinity. These narratives

1. Kaplan, trans., *The Seven Beggars*, 121.

describe human beings with a transcendent purpose, and that being human has always been complex and difficult.

For the last fifty years, the Hebrew Bible has been at the very center of my professional life as a rabbi and university professor. This text remains a daily referent in my personal studies and continues to provoke me to think, discuss, study, and write. The Hebrew Bible contains the Five Books of Moses, Prophets, and Writings. It became the dynamic source for rabbinic interpretation and commentary, and the process from which ultimately a non-biblical Judaism emerged—a religion that was created without priests, sacrifices, the Temple, or prophets—for a community living in the Diaspora.

Much of the Hebrew Bible is included in the Christian Bible, where it is often referred to as the Old Testament. As a Jew, I don't refer to these texts as the Old Testament because they are my *only* testament. The three great Western monotheistic religious traditions share these texts and continue to draw wisdom from them today.

Jewish tradition has always permitted and encouraged interpretation of the biblical text. The rabbis believed that once the Torah was given at Sinai, the text became humanity's responsibility. Decades of Jewish interpretation created an entire literary genre: *midrash*. We continue to expect that any ambiguity in the Hebrew Bible will be enlarged, illuminated, and developed into new ideas. I do not offer my reading and interpretation of the Hebrew Bible as superior or authoritative, nor a rejection of what others understand. But I do hope that the book you are now reading will stand in this long tradition of engaging this ancient text.

Jewish tradition encourages linking the ancient text to our own lives. The rabbis of each generation feel it is their obligation to explain what the text means now as we are reading it, rather than merely repeating what it has meant to earlier generations. I naturally consider the context from within which I am studying and teaching as the most important link I can connect. The questions I find within the text have been asked before, but the current context is immediate and completely mine. My goal is to bring together the ancient texts and our current reality and to elaborate on the conversation between them.

Every text has its own context: the complex historical and cultural realities behind the text. Every reader brings her immediate context to the act of reading the text. Interpretation of texts requires the critical discernment of how the different contexts distort meanings. Understanding a text comes only when we have carefully considered the many different meanings and distortions we find in our critical reading. When the text is biblical, our task is even more complex.

The Hebrew Bible is the unique source of wisdom, instruction, and history in which I continue to find myself. While it is an ancient and sometimes problematic source, this is *the text* that I can study alone and share with others. The Hebrew Bible is an inexhaustible spiritual experience of learning and reflection. A person need not believe and accept the religious assertions in the Bible in order to read it critically and engage in the serious questions it raises.

The Defining Characteristics of Judaism

There are three primary and defining characteristics of Judaism: God, Torah, and Israel. They are each necessary elements of the textual, liturgical, philosophical, and sociological identity of Jews. And yet, they each carry a universal meaning that can apply regardless of our religious tradition.

God

The Hebrew Bible is an ancient text about God. The stories about people and events serve to make the inaccessible topic of God more accessible. The Bible recounts the beginning of human belief in the Single Unseen and Unseeable Divine source of creation, redemption, and revelation. This move to ethical monotheism is, in my view, the most significant paradigm shift in the development of religion in the Western culture. God is the force for purposeful life; God is the source of moral direction and ritual piety; God is the transcendent vision that sustains humanity's ability to hope and strive.

I was sixteen when I came to this realization after a simple surgery on my left knee. The surgery was calamitous, and I went into post-surgical shock and was rushed back to the hospital with staph infection and gangrene. I overheard the melodramatic conversation between the doctor and my parents. My life was threatened, and even if they *could* save me, I might need to have my leg amputated from my mid-thigh. I would remain in isolation until they could be sure. No one ever talked to me, even though everyone was talking about me.

I stayed up all night, as they came in every hour-on-the-hour to deal with the infected surgical wound. They controlled my pain, but no one made any effort to control my imagination. I was not afraid of death but was very angry about dying. With adolescent certainty, I already doubted the existence of God and had not yet fully appreciated my own life's purpose.

I visualized the ocean waves that I had grown up watching near my home and being drawn to the feeling of certainty that image provided me. After some time, I concluded that no matter what happened to me, the waves would always be present. This simple but profound truth helped me to accept the inherent limits of being human and to begin to reflect on the mysteries that lie beyond human understanding. The sun rose that morning, and after two more surgeries and forty-seven days of recovery, the transformed sixteen-year-old left the hospital.

The teenager who returned to high school was no longer satisfied by certainties. My experience led me to think and read about what I could not understand. Questions that had no ready-made answers fascinated me. My leg had healed but I kept wondering about what had happened. From then onward, I knew that there must be more to existence than I can explain.

Rabbi Menachem Mendel of Kotzk, a nineteenth-century sage, is thought to have taught that anyone on any street corner who could explain God fully has a version of God not worth believing. In other words, God is necessarily inexplicable. I am limited in my understanding and perspective about the Divine because I am human. Being human limits me but as such, frees me to be as human as I can! For this twenty-first-century Jew, rabbi, professor, author, *God is,* and I continue to embrace the Mystery. I do not want to have an explanation of God, because any such explanation is a human—limited, flawed, superficial— point of view of the Mystery.

Torah

Torah is much more than the Five Books of Moses or the Law, much more than a sacred scroll with garments and a crown! In Hebrew, *Torah* means teaching. At Sinai, the God who freed the slaves for service taught them how to serve—ritually and ethically. The Torah, rooted in that Sinai teaching, includes narratives and command- ments, laws and teaching, history and poetry. The text is linked to the ancient biblical experience of Israelite monotheism. There are 613 commandments directly related to the ancient sacrificial cult and biblical social structure. Many of these commandments have nothing to do with what Judaism became as a post-biblical religion. And so, we must find another meaning for Torah.

Torah as one of the three defining characteristics of Judaism means the depth and breadth of textual Judaism. The additional two elements of the Hebrew Bible, namely the Prophets and the Writings, complete the twenty-four books. The process of can- onization—editorial collection and revision—took centuries. Following the biblical period, rabbis from many different periods interpreted the biblical texts in order to derive the observances needed for Jewish life in the Diaspora—the dispersion of Jews after the fall of Jerusalem in 70 CE. The rabbinic literature was legal, ethical, and homiletical, creating entirely new texts, commentar- ies, supra-commentaries, which then required subsequent collec- tions and codification.

Torah, as a defining characteristic, is the ongoing pulse within Jews, Judaism, and the Jewish culture of writing, reflecting, commenting, and editing. We move from the Hebrew Bible, *Tanakh*, to the *Mishnah* and then *Gemara*, which together become the *Talmud*. Each generation of Jews, spread throughout an always changing Western culture, creates philosophy, new commentary, and then new law and then more commentary, specific to that generation and its social needs. Torah is not limited to a unique text, but rather is an initial text which invites and provokes each generation's own response.

Israel

Israel is the final defining characteristic, and the most complex of the three. Israel was initially the second name of the patriarch Jacob, "he who struggled with *El*/God" (Genesis 35). In Exodus 1, the name of Jacob is used to refer to his sons: *Beni Israel,* but this same idiom is used in Exod 1:7 to refer to the community of Israelites. For the rest of the Torah, this name is a communal not an individual name. While we often think of "Israel" as a country today, there is no specific use of the term in Scripture to reference the land where Moses is leading the people. Rather, the land is called "the land promised for the people of Israel" and often described by boundaries of other countries. After Joshua's conquest of this land, now divided into tribal inheritance, there is no single name given.

During the united monarchies of Saul, David, and Solomon, the northern collection of tribes was called the kingdom of Israel and the southern area with the capital of Jerusalem was called the kingdom of Judah. These terms continued for the remainder of the Hebrew Bible until Rome destroyed Jerusalem and exiled the people into a Diaspora that lasted until 1948. During this period, the name most often used for the region was Palestine. As the modern expression of Jewish nationhood emerged, the term the Land of Israel was consciously used by Jews. In 1948 when the State of Israel was established, the name was legally and permanently established.

Today, Jew is the term used to refer to the global collective of people who identify with the religious observances identified as Judaism and also the cultural, historical, and political categories understood as Jewish. The people who are citizens of the nation, State of Israel, are Israelis. There are no more Israelites; they ceased to exist during biblical times. The idiom "People of Israel" can be used in the liturgy or literature as a reference to all Jews in history.

Hence, Israel, as a defining characteristic, cannot be easily defined or critically described. I understand it to mean the "community" of Jews of which I am a part. Normative Jewish theology emphasizes the community over the individual; my destiny is essentially interwoven into the redemption of the community. My role and responsibility as an individual is my participation in the communal efforts, observances, and yearnings for *Tikkun Olam*, the repair of the world!

God, Torah, and Israel are the threads that run through each period of Jewish history and culture that have evolved from the Bible into contemporary life. They are not static but dynamic terms that require critical care in their use and understanding.

Missing Characteristics

"What am I missing?" is how we can critically question ourselves about life's struggles and the nature of being human. I have used this question over the years when studying and teaching the Hebrew Bible. There are six biblical figures who help us better understand ourselves because they, too, are missing something: Abraham, Rachel, Moses, Miriam, David, and Esther. Each of these biblical characters is unique and provokes endless questions for our considerations and conversations. We learn from them that the human condition has always been a struggle of being unfinished, incomplete, and imperfect.

Abraham and Rachel are the originators of the monotheism that challenged the ancient practice of polytheism and idolatry, and would eventually give birth to Judaism, Christianity, and Islam. Abraham is the first patriarch, called by the rabbis *Avinu*, our Father—the progenitor of the people. Rachel, the last matriarch, is called *Emaynu*, our Mother—the source of the people's emotional sustenance.

Moses and Miriam are the leaders, conflicted prophets, who lead the people from servitude into the service of the Unseen Unseeable Covenanting God. They are the unique siblings who emerge from Egyptian slavery and become the leaders whom the people follow. Moses is called by the rabbis, *Rabbenu*, our rabbi—our teacher and master. Miriam is called *Navi'aynu*—our prophet. Though Miriam is considered a prophet, I would also include her as *Rabbenu*, our rabbi, for in the twenty-first century, women are and should be recognized as such.

David and Esther are biblical monarchs from different periods and biblical experiences. David the adolescent warrior, poet-musician, and finally King, was entitled to everything but always unsatisfied. Esther, the main character of a Persian folktale that becomes the basis of a diaspora legend of Jewish survival and revenge. David is called by the rabbis *Ha-Melech*, the King,[2] though not the first, but the King from whom the Messiah is destined. Esther, *Ha-Malkah,* the Queen, the only such figure in the entire Hebrew Bible, without whom at least one ancient Jewish community would have been destroyed.

The three defining characteristics of Jewish identity: God, Torah, and Israel, with the critical template, "What am I missing?" leads us to an unexpected conclusion. Though these six biblical characters are exceptionally important, maybe even paradigmatic for the Hebrew Bible, each pair is missing one of the defining elements.

Abraham and Rachel are founders of monotheism, the single God, who promises through their families, Israel—both the people and land—that they will become a great nation as great as the stars

---

2. In Hebrew, the idiom, *Ha-Melech*, is correctly translated as The King, but there is no correct way to convey the inclusion of the definite article in English. Therefore, I have chosen to capitalize King and Queen to convey the Hebrew's additional emphasis.

in the sky, yet both are missing Torah. The patriarchs and matriarchs precede God's unique revelatory presence at Mt. Sinai.

Moses and Miriam are both intimate with God, and bring the freed slaves to Mt. Sinai for the revelation of Torah. Yet, neither completes the journey to the Promised Land—Israel—and both die in the wilderness.

King David unites the tribes and rules over more land than anyone, and the prophet Nathan is his generation's source of Torah. But when David asks to build the Temple for God, he is forbidden. Esther, a Jewish Queen in the Diaspora, has the power to save the Jewish community from disaster. Yet, the Scroll of Esther that tells her story never mentions God, so like David, she too is missing a defining characteristic.

These six extraordinary biblical figures are all missing a defining characteristic, yet none are any less essential. The text of the Hebrew Bible is teaching us a profound truth about being human. We are all missing a defining element of our own identity. None of us is perfect, and no one has it all! Being human is about learning what is missing and living a meaningful life accepting our basic human condition.

For some, the quest for perfection defies very real limits of time. Abraham and Rachel were limited by their historical circumstances; they were missing Torah because they were living at the wrong time. Like them, many of us chase the memories of a past that is gone or the imagined dreams of a future that cannot be reached. Moses and Miriam were limited by the very community to whom they were sent and, ultimately, missed reaching the land where they were leading their people. Like them, many of us ignore our own humanity and the many complex realities that define us, no matter how much we deny it. David and Esther, who exemplify the difficulty of holding and using power, missed God's transcendent presence. Like them, many of us strive for power only to misunderstand the power we have or abuse the power we achieve.

We are all missing a defining element. We all need this or that missing puzzle piece in order to feel complete. Sometimes in our searching we forget to ask ourselves the most difficult questions. Elie Wiesel teaches:

> It is our ability to ask certain questions which make us what we are, human or not. Answers divide people; questions unite them. The questions which we ask fill us with some measure of humility when we are confronted by events that transcend us. Not to ask would make us into slaves. To ask gives us freedom.[3]

3. Heuck, "Elie Wiesel," 12.

3

Abraham: Empathy and the Importance of Just Ten Good People

E very clergy person has a story about a person who came in
from the very cold or very hot and sat down for a hot or
cold beverage and maybe an unexpected sweet something. We
all see the homeless, hungry, and lost souls in today's cities, but
churches, synagogues, and mosques of every kind welcome them.
Such a person was "John" who came regularly to my synagogue
to find refuge especially from the bitter winter. He came to our
Saturday morning Torah (Bible) study, where there was hot water
and some treats from the previous night's Sabbath reception. He
rarely spoke, sitting in a corner listening and being grateful for the
refuge. Eventually some members came to me and expressed their
concern for him and suggested we try to help. John did not want
us to take him to a shelter or give him money. He just wanted
to sit, listen, and have his hot water, though over time people
brought him coffee and a roll.

The clergy talked with him, trying to learn his story, and
asked how they could help, but his quiet presence did not offer
up details or constructive suggestions. One day during a bitter
winter storm, the police called the synagogue to inform us that
John had died. He froze to death during the night and they found
one of the rabbis' card in his pocket. The congregation provided

John a plot in our cemetery, paid for a simple burial, and all of our clergy performed his funeral in front of a hand full of people. John taught me that really caring about a person sleeping outside under a highway requires more than looking out my car window and asking, "What can I do?"

The Bible recounts the narrative of the Hebrews who began an entirely new way of life: ethical monotheism. The radical shift from polytheism and idolatry is never explained but is modeled through the lives of Abraham, Sarah, and their family. The text does not provide us with an explanation of how monotheism developed, of its superiority to polytheism, or of why Abraham was chosen as its first agent.

Gen 11:26–32[1] provides a very brief summary of Abraham's background. The Hebrews are refugees from ancient Mesopotamia, near today's Iraq. Abraham's identity as a monotheist begins with a *divine* call to leave his father's family and go on his own to Canaan. Later rabbinic interpreters (third to fifth century CE) provided their own interpretations of the backstory to Abraham's father, Terach:

R. Hiyya said:

Abraham's father, Terach, was an idol manufacturer. Once he had to travel, so he left Abraham to manage the shop. Abraham took a hammer in his hand, broke all the idols to pieces, and then put the hammer in the hand of the biggest idol among them. When his father came back and saw the broken idols, he was appalled. "Who did this?" he cried. "How can I hide anything from you?" replied Abraham calmly, ". . . the biggest one got up, took the hammer and broke all the others to pieces." "What are you trying to pull on me?" asked Terach, "Do they have minds?" Said Abraham: "Listen to what your own mouth is saying? They have no power at all! Why worship idols?"[2]

1. Berlin and Breitler, *The Jewish Study Bible.* All biblical chapter and verse references throughout are from this source.

2. "*Midrash Rabbah, Bereishit Rabbah* 38:13."

This famous story was created to explain how and why Abraham came to understand the rational necessity of belief in one God rather than many idols. Even though it comes completely from the imagination of ancient rabbinic scholars, it makes so much sense that many Jewish children who learn it are shocked when they find out it is not in the Bible!

We cannot imagine these first monotheists, nor their life struggles of infertility, famine, and violence. By choosing to follow the Unique God, they become Western culture's first religious immigrants, seeking a new place in which to live and practice a still-evolving religious identity. This family of nomadic immigrants likely never imagined the religious history of Western culture, and that one day Abraham would be invoked by Jews, Christians, and Muslims.

The Hebrews all shared a common experience: their One God negated the social and cultural worship of idols but provided humans a unique relationship. Abraham had no previous model of monotheism, no Scripture, and no rituals. The biblical text describes him following God with complete and utter faithfulness— even in cases that any modern reader would find horrific. For example, his willingness to sacrifice his son, Isaac, on an altar in Genesis 22. The story of the near-sacrifice of Isaac is one of many reminders that the Bible is an ancient text that must be carefully interpreted by the modern reader. Scholars have explained that this chapter was probably used to express the Hebrews' prohibition of human sacrifice!

Throughout Abraham's life and the lives of the generations that follow him, the Single Unseen God affirms that each generation of this clan is a model for others. Genesis 12–50 describes the universal dynamics of marriage, children, siblings, infertility, jealousy, competition, secrecy, and reconciliation. These are stories of hope, regardless of the suffering; they offer the Bible's first expressions of faith. It is in these biblical texts that we learn the expected ethical behavior long before the commandments are given. The experience of the covenantal relationship with God is our source for how to understand our purpose and our ethics. Each of the patriarchs and matriarchs models that human relationships, like the relationship with the Single Unseen God, require engagement.

One of the more complex examples is when Abraham's infertile wife, Sarah, offers her maid, Hagar, to her husband as a surrogate. Abraham accepts Sarah's offer and Abraham has his first son. Later, Sarah becomes jealous and asks that Hagar and Ishmael be sent away. Their expulsion is shocking and starkly painful; the biblical text teaches that being human is not simple and that ethics are often learned in lessons that should not be repeated.

The biblical text's most dramatic affirmation of empathy and rejection of indifference is Abraham's argument with God over the destruction of Sodom. Suddenly in Genesis 18, God determines that humans have again degraded an unstated limit of evil. There is no textual explanation as to why the punishment is deserved, but when God shares this determination with Abraham, he challenges the Divine for the sake of just ten righteous persons. Gen 18:22-33 is an extraordinary example of dialogue and debate between humanity and the Divine. Abraham intercedes, illustrating the need for humans to ethically engage on behalf of even those judged to be unacceptable.

The text is profound. "What if there are fifty, then forty, thirty, twenty, even ten innocents *within the city*, should the innocent be destroyed among the wicked?" The use of *"within the city"* permits us to measure righteousness by even the most complex realities of being human. Even the ancients understood that being righteous was the most difficult when people live among other people. "Far be it from You to do such a thing, to bring death upon the innocent as well as the guilty" (Gen 18:25). Abraham assumes that monotheism and its covenantal relationship provide an ethical challenge even to God. Biblical ethics permit no equivocation about indifference. Being a bystander is unacceptable.

Many people read the biblical text of Genesis 18 as a condemnation of homosexuality, hence the origin of the word, sodomy. But, a passage in Ezekiel 16 has been used by many biblical interpreters to suggest that Sodom was actually the most inhospitable community in the ancient world—so the sin of Sodom is more about hospitality than sexuality. The people had so many blessings, yet they refused to share any of them, especially with outsiders. The ancient rabbis emphasized the community's cruelty, rejection of all differences, and its arrogance about anyone in need.

One particular ancient legend tells of a young girl who secretly fed a poor man with bread she hid in her water jug. After three days of searching for the person feeding the beggar, Sodom's residents found the girl. The leaders of Sodom left her on top of the city walls covered in honey so everyone would see her as the bees came to destroy her. The ancient rabbis say it was her cries of pain that God heard and decided that Sodom was so evil that no repentance was possible.

Abraham does not have the Torah, the revelation of God's commandments; yet he argues with God that even Sodom must be evaluated for the sake of ten good people. If monotheism requires humans to care about one another, then God too must be held to the ethical impulse of empathy. Even though there were not ten righteous people, the debate with God remains valid because even one person was willing to engage for the sake of the Other.

Though Abraham is missing an essential defining characteristic of Jewish life, the Torah, his life models the ethical impulse of engagement in the suffering of others. This is a timeless lesson about human nature: we are uniquely connected to each other; being human requires caring! We all think about the universal code of the Golden Rule, the source of which is given in Leviticus 19—love your neighbor as yourself, an ethic shared by all monotheistic faiths. The first monotheists lived by this before God commanded it.

In my lifetime, one unique challenge of disease and death that continues to test this fundamental ethical assertion is HIV/AIDS. As of this writing, the latest published statistics of the global pandemic are difficult to completely fathom:

- 77.3 million [59.9 million–100 million] people have become infected with HIV since the start of the pandemic in 1981.

- 35.4 million [25.0 million–49.9 million] people have died from AIDS-related illnesses since the start of the pandemic in 1981.

- 36.9 million [31.1 million–43.9 million] people globally were living with HIV. The first communities infected were gay men, IV drug users, and women of color—especially in Africa among the most marginalized in every society.[3]

If we read the story of Sodom to be about exclusion, rejection, and stigmatization, then HIV/AIDS should always remind us of Abraham's argument with God. In 1986, before HIV/AIDS had become global news, I was challenged both as a rabbi and human when a young woman asked to me to visit her brother. He was in the intensive care unit with pneumocystis pneumonia (PCP), a serious illness caused by the virus. I asked if her family had a congregation and was told that her rabbi said there is no place for your brother in Judaism. I was shocked. It was during the first days of Hanukah, the Jewish festival of lights. Of course I would visit him!

Richard was the first of many individuals with HIV/AIDS that transformed me. I remember that he was weak and frail, but warmly thanked me for coming. I gave him candles for his Hanukkah menorah. He worked at the main branch of the Chicago library specializing in American folk art. His home was filled with the wonderful quilts. We spoke of his illness only briefly, and as it was getting dark, I suggested we light the Hanukah candles together.

I had only been there a little more than thirty minutes, but he said he was getting very tired and asked if I would please come back. I said of course, walked to the door, and after I put on my coat, he extended his hand to me in gratitude. For a single horrific nanosecond, my hand seemed frozen, and I did nothing. Richard quietly, gently, extended his hand closer. Finally, I engaged in a handshake of shared acknowledgement. I was terribly embarrassed and don't remember if I said anything as I left. This was the first person living with AIDS that I touched, and I was afraid of

3. "AIDSinfo," *UNAIDS*.

the disease that was killing thousands. This was my first experience with anyone who was stigmatized by the disease, but he understood my fear, and trusted himself enough to extend his hand to me as my teacher.

I remember getting into my car and sitting in the dark on that cold Chicago evening crying, screaming, and cursing about that terrible nanosecond of non-response, for being a bystander! Richard was a messenger from on High, and he gave me missing pieces to my life's puzzle. This experience initiated my engagement into the world of HIV/AIDS, a world that I embraced as an intentional act of *teshuva*, repentance, for that single horrific experience of indifference for which I will always be ashamed. Richard and I never spoke of my initial inability to accept his hand. When meeting a person living with HIV/AIDS, I have never again hesitated. I always extend my hand or embrace them if they are willing.

I visited Richard several times, eventually meeting his mother and sister. I sat with the three of them in his hospice room, six months later, holding Richard's hand as he was dying. I helped him to say the *Sh'm*a, "Hear O Israel, the Eternal Our God, the Eternal is One." This was early 1987 and the Jewish funeral home tried to require an expensive internal steel casket to prevent the spread of the virus. The medical examiner explained that this was unnecessary. Richard's mother, a nurse in a public high school, lied that her son died of cancer because she was warned that if the parents of her school knew that she had touched a person who died of AIDS she could lose her job.

All of these painful experiences faded over time as HIV/AIDS moved from panic to pandemic, from the most marginalized to the most normative. Richard's simple but profound example of extending his hand to me was a prophetic model that until this day remains as an anchor of hope. I had the necessary experience of a person, a relationship, of knowing a son and brother, not just a gay man with a disease. Richard taught me much more than to take the hand of a person with HIV/AIDS. He was my most important ethics teacher. His life was the model of what is required in being present to the person and seeing the face of anyone with this disease.

Now more than thirty years after my first encounter with HIV/AIDS, Richard, the man, artist, and friend, is the face I always put on the global pandemic; otherwise, these statistics are disorienting: nearly eighty million people have been infected and thirty-eight million have died. There is still no science or technology that offers us a vaccine or cure. The pandemic continues to challenge our racism and homophobia, and our unconscious acceptance that some people are actually "surplus populations."

Today, global institutions responsible for the increased demands for funding report an "oppressive complacency" to help especially the marginalized communities. After all this time, far too many people can dismiss this human disaster by using the categories of sin and self-destruction. The exceptional urgency has faded. More people can live with the virus as a chronic illness. Even though millions more are infected and die every year, we are either indifferent or exhausted by all of the competing ethical challenges.

Abraham is still healing from his self-performed adult circumcision when Genesis 18 opens. Three "messengers" approach his nomadic camp and Abraham immediately greets his guests with an expression of hospitality. The text says he *ran* to organize a meal for his unannounced guests. The rabbis teach us that his behavior prompts the miracle of Sarah's pregnancy of a son. For any reader today, a ninety-year-old woman conceiving a child is beyond all reasonable belief. But from the biblical context, the extraordinary act was Abraham's complete engagement with strangers coming to his home. Only later do we realize that Abraham's genuine kindness is meant to illuminate Sodom's cruelty and total lack of hospitality.

Abraham was the first to model a relationship with One God, for which his clan is promised a unique role in history. Genesis portrays this faithful nomadic people as willing to sustain their families' destiny regardless of their struggles. Is there an Abraham in our world today, a courageous visionary to remind us that even for the sake of ten righteous people living with

AIDS, we must not look away? Have we lost the empathy taught by these first monotheists, that every individual is precious to the Single Unseen and Unseeable God?

Abraham, the ancient nomad, somehow understood that clay idols could not help humans be fully human. The biblical challenges faced by the patriarchs and matriarchs are no longer issues in the twenty-first century. Science and technology have created solutions for famine and infertility, but we continue to face violence from people dissatisfied with their boundaries or their tribal pride. When we look back at the limited scope of Abraham's life with a perspective of four thousand years of progress, we are even more amazed at his very sophisticated ability to think, behave, and engage others. The primary ethical impulse of the monotheism that has developed into Judaism, Christianity, and Islam has its deepest roots in these biblical passages and in the model of this first monotheist.

Anyone who takes the time to express concern about human issues today will be quickly overwhelmed. The obvious crisis of homelessness and poverty in our urban areas is so vast that some communities have given up and tent cities have become the norm along highways. Hunger and obesity are both public health crises. As we live and move through our cities and towns, it is inevitable to encounter humans and their tragic burdens, but these issues have been politicized, and then polarized, and finally easily dismissed.

Our ethical impulse has been flattened by the intense political discourse. We are overstimulated by a never-ending flow of information. Do we see the failures of policies or the waste of welfare when we lose our ability or willingness to see these people as humans like ourselves? The complexity of our world's crises makes it impossible for a single person to engage with genuine concern.

The world has not yet been able to share a common response to the urgent demands of climate change, and again, the political rage on both sides makes it easy to dismiss. There are more than sixty-five million refugees globally, an issue that has profoundly polarized several nations politically. These are only two of the most obvious crises that would surely overwhelm even an Abraham. The task of engagement must begin with the simple and daily commitment to make a difference in just one person's life.

Maybe it is the unsolicited kindness offered to a stranger, or a long-forgotten note to a friend, or an expression of gratitude to a person who is always there and rarely seen—like a custodian, doorman, or toll booth attendant. The lonely experience of life is the systemic reality of far too many people. We argue about bullies even as we ignore people in our presence. None of us are prophetic religious leaders who hear the voice God (or likely, we are not), but all of us are capable of showing the hospitality of Abraham when strangers come into our presence. None of us will be held accountable for arguing on behalf of a city's fate, but all of us can speak out about the fate of our neighborhood's park, or playground, or traffic lights.

Abraham is the Hebrew Bible's first religious hero and model of what the three Western monotheistic faiths might become. Abraham's life story is surely worth more reflection and interpretation, especially because he is presented as incomplete, missing one of the essential elements that defines monotheistic religion: revealed Scripture. Our most enduring example of a human being who experienced the Undefinable reality of God was missing something because he was the first. The Bible offers us a model that is completely human so we can find ourselves in his story and his questions. We should not follow all of Abraham's examples, but we should struggle to challenge ourselves to be more open to those whose suffering should not be ignored.

Our lives will not be measured like biblical characters who are beyond our historical standards and outside our social norms, but by the daily acts of ethical concern that make a difference for only one other person. We cannot solve poverty, hunger, illiteracy, or opioid addiction, but we can model a genuine willingness to be present and engaged with someone who needs our help. The biblical texts about the first monotheist, Abraham, provide an example of a human who heard the Divine offer to challenge history and never be indifferent to another person's suffering.

4

Rachel: *Only* One God Requires Religious Pluralism

You always begin the same way every time you have to make a decision. You are going to purchase something, visit somewhere, move somewhere, choose a university, or pick a candidate for an elected office. You read some material, you try to learn, drive, visit, or taste so you can have an experience that helps with your decision. You read some more, especially reviews by others, then you begin measuring costs to value to determine if you can get a good deal. You are getting ready to make your choice and you take the risk of discussing your ideas and points of view with others you trust. Sometimes you feel affirmed, but at other times you are surprised when you have to defend your decision.

You use all of your contacts, review all of your input and you do it, buy it, choose it—move, say yes, say no—whatever is needed! You are pleased, maybe even proud. Then, somewhat unexpectedly, someone asks you why you didn't read or hear other apparently obvious sources or points of view. Your confidence is high, and your response is calm. Yes, I read it, or it was only a rumor. After a few weeks or maybe a few months, you are becoming weary of explaining yourself; you were so sure, you had really done your homework this time, but there is a small but strong group of Others who think you are wrong. Suddenly, without thinking about the ramifications, you begin to explain your decision with a new certainty anchored in your rejection of any other option. Any other car that was not made in the US, any other clothes that were made by child labor in Asia. Any other food is surely filled with fat, sugar, and chemical preservatives. The university you chose has diversity and every other university is shutting down free speech or is spending more on athletics than on academics.

We all know how this shift unravels. We had to make a choice and our choice felt good. But when others began questioning the decision, suddenly the choice was defended by rejecting every other option. There were many different possibilities, whether cars, universities, clothes, food, doctors, or candidates, but after trying to hold on to your choice, you realize that rejection is easier than explaining your choice over and over. Advertising, competition, social media, even simple tribal-like divisions of sports all feed this process of a positive choice for something being turned into an aggressive decision against any other possibility.

The Hebrew Bible's position on polytheism and idolatry seems to follow this pattern. The Unique Unseen and Unseeable God establishes a covenant with the Hebrews, and without any explanation, it forbids any other form of worship. Only later does the biblical text make clear through commandments the total opposition to any form of idolatry. The narrative of the Golden Calf[1] illustrates this sin especially after the Exodus and revelation of the Torah on Mt. Sinai. The social and religious world of the Hebrew Bible is complex and the attempt to establish monotheism was difficult, so it is understandable that there is no partial acceptance of the polytheism of other cultures.

There is no greater danger to the commitment to the One and Only God than idolatry, which is why idolatry is the worst sin in the Hebrew Bible. Yet, this understandable obsession with the exclusion of any other religious experience has historically created a tragic paradox. Each of the Western monotheistic faiths produced an understanding that their relationship with God was exclusive. In other words, Judaism, Christianity, and Islam each teach that

---

1. Golden Calf requires capitalization because the rabbis give this biblical text an idiomatic name, *Egel HaZahav*. The translation is best conveyed by capitalizing Golden Calf.

the Unique[2] God has called each of them to be God's sacred community in love and obedience.

The exclusive, singular relationship that each monotheistic faith has with the Only God creates the belief that any other faith is wrong and must be excluded. Thus, each monotheism tragically teaches that it is exclusively true, and others must be rejected. Though all Jews, Christians, and Muslims share a common textual origin and agree that they all have the same Divine[3] source, they intentionally interpret the same texts so that only *their* community is the true and final recipient of God's blessing. Historically, each claim with complete certainty that only their specific relationship with the One and Only God is *the* means of redemption, salvation, and communal perfection.

What am I missing? The One universal God, shared by the three Western scriptural faiths, offers each an exclusive relationship which must also exclude the others. Human nature determines that our choice, even of God, is finally determined by the exclusion of all other expressions of religious experience. Yet, it is time to reject exclusive statements of belief: I alone have all the truth, and anyone who differs is abandoned by the grace of God.

The final matriarch and Jacob's most beloved, Rachel, teaches us that each individual is unique, not merely another link in the clan, not simply another wife or mother. The biblical story of Rachel offers us an important lesson about pluralism, the equality of diverse realities within a single community.

Jacob goes back to *Padan Aram*, the clan's original community, and finds Rachel. Her father, Laban, Jacob's uncle, requires labor and integration into the community before Jacob can have his wife. Laban uses secrecy and manipulation to force Jacob to unwittingly marry Leah, the older sister. Only after he marries Leah can he

---

2. The Hebrew term, *Kodesh*, is poorly translated as Holy but actually means Unique, set apart from all other things. I use the capitalized Unique to emphasize the power of singularity in God which we experience as holiness.

3. As previously noted about Unique, the capitalized Divine emphasizes the biblical experience of God. Using an English word with a capital 'D' makes the reader stop and think about the word as much more than an adjective, but a spiritual reality beyond our mere grammatical rules.

marry the woman he loves, Rachel. Rachel and Leah are the only sisters who marry the same man and each shares their maid with Jacob as well. Rachel's infertility motivates her to facilitate Jacob sharing four women as the mothers of "*Bnei Israel*—the children of Israel." Unlike Sarah, who has Hagar and Ishmael expelled, *all* of Jacob's sons are integrated into a single clan family.

Finally, Rachel gives birth to Joseph, the son who becomes Jacob's favorite child. Rachel's second son, Benjamin, is the last son born to a matriarch. The only matriarch to die during childbirth (Gen 35:16-21), she is buried in between Jerusalem and Bethle- hem—in Hebron, in the *Cave of the Machpelah*—and the only one not to be buried with the rest of the patriarchs and matriarchs. Though Rachel, the most loved of the four women, has only two sons, it is her presence that links all of the mothers of the children. Through her life, the plurality of the twelve tribes of Israel comes to be. Her life represents pluralism: multiple life paths, relation- ships, identities, and finally legacies.

The rabbinic legends emphasized that Rachel's empathy can be traced to her family. Though Rachel was deeply in love with Jacob, she helps spare her older sister from the shame of being unmarried and deceives Jacob. His love for her only motivates him to work more to earn his promised rights of Rachel. Jacob's absolute love for Rachel hurts Leah, who ultimately becomes the most fertile while Rachel remains infertile. This one polygamous patriarchal family involves two sisters and their two maids, but only Rachel struggles with both jealousy and infertility.

The rabbis understand that Rachel represents a different kind of biblical figure, requiring interpretations to explain her legacy as the Mother of Israel. It is this image of Rachel, as the ultimate "mother" figure, that the prophet Jeremiah uses when he refers to Rachel sobbing as the Israelites go into Exile: "Thus said the Lord: A cry is heard in Ramah—Wailing bitter weeping—Rachel weep- ing for her children. She refuses to be comforted for her children, who are gone . . . " (Jer 31:15-16).

The rabbis teach that all the patriarchs and even Moses plead with God about the Exile, but it is only the tears of Rachel, *Emaynu,*

Our Mother, that get God's attention and response: "Your children shall return to their country." Rachel is never silent, passive, or uncaring when the People of Israel[4] walk past her grave. She remains the model of an individual who embraces her family, the clan, as the community. Even today, infertile women go to the site of her grave outside of Jerusalem to pray that Rachel, the Mother of Israel, will hear their tears to help them as women.

Rachel teaches us about social and cultural pluralism when she asks her nephew, Ruben, for the mandrakes he found. These plants were believed to have potent powers that Rachel wanted to use because of her infertility. She offered her sister, Leah, the right to be with Jacob in order to get the plants' benefit. The biblical text reaffirms that only God could remember her, yet the fact that we find this passage suggests that the final editors want us to know of the many ways women chose to respond to their yearning for survival. Rachel understands that the covenant with the Unique God requires another generation. Jacob had other sons, but she alone had provided none. Maybe the "mandrakes" are a necessary reminder that women carry a unique power of fertility and guilt of infertility.

Finally, the Rachel narrative includes the clan's assimilation into the dominant culture of *Padan Aram*. The text states, ". . . and Rachel stole her father's household idols" (Gen 31:19b). Laban confronts her, and she lies to her father while sitting on top of the idols, saying that she cannot get up because "the way of women is upon me." The biblical text leaves the reader with questions about Laban and even Rachel's use of the idols. There are some biblical scholars who argue that this text reflects a period in which monotheism was still evolving. Maybe Rachel's struggle with being beautiful and loved but infertile leads her to share in an older social and religious assimilation. I believe that her role in Genesis is to teach that pluralism, being open and respectful of different paths, has always been essential to monotheism.

---

4. Capitalizing People of Israel is my attempt to convey the Hebrew idiom, *Am Israel*, used in rabbinic literature. This is an important term of the nation that still remained a collective even in exile.

Ancient conflicts over who is the most loved by the Universal One God are still stimulating hatred. Tragically, this distortion has proven to be a dangerously intractable idea, and today fuels inter-religious competition and politicized religious extremism. Here is what we are missing in our interfaith dialogues: The task of *each* human, of *every* human, is to affirm the world in which he or she is present for God's sake. We cannot affirm *for ourselves* unless we are secure in affirming for *everyone else.*

There are painful lessons we cannot learn from texts nor teachers but only from the experiences of a "puzzle-piece" rela-tionship in life. The first time I was called a "Christ Killer," I was seven years old. The boy who lived across the street came home from his catechism class and I had been waiting to play baseball with him and another friend. Each one of us had something, one had a ball, one had a glove, and one had a bat. He said, because you are a Christ Killer, we could not play together anymore. For the first time in my life I was unacceptable for being a Jew. It was 1953, fourteen years before the Catholic Church would change its teaching about Judaism with the publication of *Nostra Aetate.*

Biblical monotheism has a simple formula—the One God re-quires an exclusive relationship that excludes all others. When God chooses your community, you are set apart in history. All mono-theistic faiths anchored in the Hebrew Bible share this mechanism of exclusivity and exclusion which tragically leads to the perverse claim that their particular form of Abraham's ancient insight is *the* superior and *final* experience of God's presence and grace.

Christianity emerged from this scriptural tradition to affirm that the exclusive love of the One God comes *only* in the unique incarnate Christ. God's salvation provides eternal life, but that love is only for those who are "reborn" by his death and blood, and not for anyone who rejects this final and absolute truth about God. The Christian Scriptures use narratives that describe those responsible for the death of Jesus—Judas the apostle, and the Judeans/Jews who yelled, "Crucify him, crucify him!" This kind of scriptural anti-Judaism breeds an antisemitism that is so em-bedded in our culture that the word "Jew" has become the only proper noun to be used as a verb: "(lowercase) *"to jew"* [offensive]: to bargain sharply and beat down in price."[5] Jews of every generation, in every country in the world, face antisemitism as a matter of personal experience.

My studies, teaching, and rabbinic work all confirm that the boy across the street had learned that I was a Christ killer from his church teachings. My commitment to Jewish-Christian dialogues has been my way to prevent any other Jewish child from having that scary experience of being called a killer of Christ!

When I retired as a congregational rabbi, I was invited to teach Jewish studies at a public state university that had settled a class action lawsuit on antisemitism and communal harassment. Perhaps the clearest evidence of antisemitism were the five swastikas built into the outside design of the Cathedral of St. Mary. After a terrible fire, the church was reconstructed between 1927 and 1931 based on a third-century cathedral in Ravenna, Italy. That historic building included the ancient symbol of the *Hakenkreuze* (or broken cross), a symbol that would later be recognized as the swastika.

5. "Jew, v.," Oxford English Dictionary Online.

Father Steve Binsfeld, the pastor of St. Mary's at that time, explained that the parish council had voted to remove the five discs containing the swastikas, but the removal and replacement would require $14,000. The parish congregation housed in the cathedral building had become small and older so that raising this amount was very difficult. I offered to help with contacts and raised $11,000. Father Binsfeld and I taught a dialogue course on the beliefs and practices of Jews and Catholics, a first in St. Cloud, Minnesota. In May 2006, five new discs were dedicated after the five containing *Hakenkreuze* swastikas were removed. The service was officiated by the Bishop, Father Binsfeld, and I, who was the first non-Christian ever to speak in the cathedral.

While it took seventy-five years for the offending symbols to be removed, should the community be judged as antisemitic for waiting? Some of the people who grew up in the church complained that it was the new Jewish professor/rabbi who raised money from Jews who took away Catholic history. Should the complex history of the symbol and its use be stained beyond acceptance because of World War II and the racist hatred of the Nazi Holocaust?

I thought about the removal of these five swastikas while four monuments/memorials of Confederate leaders were removed after nearly 150 years in New Orleans. The African American community had expressed its communal frustration and pain over the indifference of the white community's refusal to acknowledge the meaning of these public statements of racism. The mayor of New Orleans explained after months of communal process why the city had taken this courageous step: "Removal of these monuments is a rejection of what was called the corner-stone of the Confederacy: the great truth, that the negro is not equal to the white man; that slavery—subordination to the superior race—is his natural and normal condition."[6]

Many people have argued that the removal of such offensive physical links to America's racist past is a form of historical revisionism. Can we teach about the past if we remove its artifacts? Regardless of the extraordinary pain Auschwitz represents, I would strongly oppose its destruction. Walking through the infamous "*Arbeit Macht Frei*" gate is a unique experience, as is walking down the train tracks that link Auschwitz and Birkenau where the gas chambers and crematoria are located. The camps exist even as we still face inexplicable Holocaust denial. One can only imagine what the deniers will say in the absence of such physical reality.

I am not an African American and I will not attempt to assert any equivalence between Confederate monuments and Nazi camps; I will not argue that my experience of antisemitism is comparable to their experience of racism. I understood that the "*Hakenkreuze*" swastikas on the Cathedral of St. Mary could be removed because the parish wanted them replaced. It was not merely

6. "Mitch Landrieu's Speech," *New York Times*.

outsiders demanding a change, and their existence was not linked with an original intent to be hurtful.

The marginalized communities of color have every right to challenge the dominant white community about the way American history must be shared if there is ever going to be reconciliation. When these artifacts of white supremacy are removed, I want them stored and then placed in a national museum of American history that openly and self-critically reviews the entire past, just as the original offensive swastikas are on display inside the church as a teaching tool.

Rabbi Menahem Mendel of Kotzk used to ask, if anyone on any street corner could explain God to you, would you want that to be your God? Thinking about it for even a few minutes might embarrass you, as if the question wants to know if you are an elitist, but the deeper issue is whether someone's explanation of God has the spiritual depth to be the Unique Eternal God. This mind experiment has taught me that when I am in dialogue with Christians and Muslims, I cannot, nor should I, try to explain their understanding of God.

Over the years, I find myself watching the faces of Catholics after they have taken Communion, trying to imagine their sense of being with God. I have listened intensely to Christians explain their personal sense of love and profound peace in knowing that God's Son died for them. Since I cannot explain God to myself, it would surely be impossible to explain it to someone who is not Jewish. Yet, I engage in serious inter-religious dialogue to understand the people, not God. I need to build respect and communal partnerships with people who share our common God, though none of us can share a common explanation nor understanding of that common God.

Our current political and social division has become murderous. The vulgarity of bigotry has become increasingly violent as white supremacists have determined that words and ideas are insufficient. Now, the most extreme need to use deathly violence to act out their rage, fear, and rejection of any difference. Race, nationality, gender, and sexual orientation are not rational choices about which there can be any arguments. Yet, we are dealing with terrorists whose distorted notions about race, religion, gender, or sexual orientation only reject people.

This universal truth of One God remains a shared yearning. But we still seem to be confused. No one is superior to anyone else, whether measured by religion, gender, race, profession, or purpose. Pluralism is a powerful ideal: we can be awed by multiple truths and engage in dialogues that open hearts and minds but claim no final conclusions. Or, we can simply dismiss pluralism as one of many great theories that can only be discussed but never really experienced.

Our current deeply divided communities are "locked and loaded" for much more immediate ethical gridlock. We feel that it is impossible to push back against those that want to define themselves by rejecting others. It is exhausting to keep arguing about immigrants, Muslims, women, transgender people, and gun-lovers.

We thought that surely the scenes of the extermination camps and the testimonies of survivors would endure for more than seventy-five years. The global increase in antisemitism cannot be explained easily. We are facing the oldest known prejudice in virulent new forms. Social media has transformed bigots into viral trolls who provoke new questions of free speech. We are using ever-expanding forms of technology without first determining their limits. Live streaming has been used to capture both racist harassment and a white supremacist's mass murder in real time.

The complexity of today's pluralism and bigotry require us to stop and be quiet sometimes. We need to be far more critical of what we hear and read. We should not engage in social discourse without picturing the person or people to whom we are speaking. Would we say the same things to a person in a face-to-face conversation? Tweets and Facebook posts are too easy; they don't require the actual experience of engagement when another person is struck by our words, tone, and emotion. We are not obligated to stop the flood of hatred in our days, but we cannot remain silent and indifferent to hatred in our presence.

Pluralism is created with the building blocks of relationships and personal experiences. Taking the risks of learning about difference through sharing our own story and listening to someone else's story. Understanding that differences in real people are the "missing pieces" of our own sense of pluralism. If we open ourselves in these experiences, then their differences can no longer be twisted into political lies that can be dismissed with our silence. We can create our own experience of pluralism, one different person at a time.

5

Miriam: The Imperfect Leader Who Danced

Leadership has become its own industry—a fifteen billion dollar global industry that adds to the already significant library of essays, lectures, videos, and books. There is always another best-seller that promises how to be a leader with "Today's Five Most Essential Truths." Yet, there is no agreement on the basic characteristics of a leader, nor a common standard by which we should measure leadership. "What am I missing?" Leadership is an industry that cannot define the product.

At this same moment, we lack global leaders who are prepared, capable, or even willing to respond with a proper sense of urgency to these crises: sixty-five million refugees, the income gap that divides the top 1 percent from everyone else, the more than one billion illiterate adults and children, and the daily death of sixteen thousand young children because they had neither clean water nor sanitation. Maybe there are no leaders today because we measure success and failure by trends on social media rather than in critical communal terms.

Today, the critical scale of leadership is determined all too often by viral YouTube hits, Twitter followers, or Reality-TV ratings. Sometimes we assume that a new thirty-year-old high-tech billionaire must have legitimate leadership skills. The CEO who significantly influences popular culture can still be challenged for his use of child labor. We continue to misunderstand that real political leadership should not be measured by funds raised rather than public engagement in ideas, and that democracy is too easily mischaracterized as style over substance.

We must note that women have been held back from leadership opportunities for decades. The US has still not elected a woman as President, and women make up only 25 percent of both the House and Senate, even though women represent 50 percent of the US population. We have achieved the highest rate of women CEOs at Fortune 500 companies with 5.4 percent, and at those same companies, 26 percent of the executive positions are filled with women. While this is certainly progress, we have a long way to go.

While bearing children and as primary parents and home managers, women still face a unique challenge in finding a place at the table of future leaders. Society imposes enormous barriers on those who try to be both leaders and women. Studies show that women are evaluated by their productivity and past behavior, while men with all the same background are more often measured by their potential—what they *might* achieve in the future. Our current global political and business cultures sustain the myths that good leaders are aggressive and risk-taking, both generally understood as masculine qualities. Among public leaders, women who act aggressively can be misunderstood as immature and unwilling to pay their dues; being forceful is interpreted as being angry or shrew-like. Women have an impossible task—to be both leaders and women.

Miriam, the older sister of Aaron and Moses, is introduced in Exodus as an entirely different kind of woman. The women in Genesis were wives and mothers; their sibling relationships were not the defining relationship of their biblical identity. Miriam, who is neither a wife nor a mother, has a significant role as a biblical leader because all the men around her relate to her as an individual woman rather than in relation to a husband or son.

In Exodus 1, two midwives, Shifra and Puah, save the Israelite infants from Pharaoh's brutal order to kill all male Israelite babies. According to rabbinic commentators, Shifra and Puah are actually Yocheved (Moses' mother) and Miriam. Neither of these women is afraid of Pharaoh's brutal decrees, but the text notes that both are "afraid of God," a term used through the Hebrew Bible as a positive description of a person's moral and spiritual values. Miriam is a woman prepared to defy a cruel oppressive ruler, even as she has reverence of the Unique Unseen God that has not yet acknowledged the suffering of the Israelites.

Moses' mother, with the help of Miriam, is determined to save her infant's life. The older sister puts her brother into the Nile River in a basket. Miriam decides that the river's edge is the right place, and chooses the exact time to place the basket carrying her still unnamed brother into the river. Miriam engages, watches, and intervenes; according to the Hebrew text, she "learns" what will happen when Pharaoh's daughter sees the infant. Miriam waits for the infant to be taken out of the water and immediately offers to help Pharaoh's daughter find a wet-nurse for the child.

Here Miriam's character teaches us about the importance of family life as an older sibling, not as a parent. According to rabbinic legend, she had even chastised her father for separating from her mother in order to prevent a baby's conception, permitting Pharaoh's decree to dissolve the family. Imagine! the rabbis teach, Miriam is not afraid of either her father or Pharaoh. She is a woman who "fears God" but not the men around her. Miriam represents a different perspective as a leader and as a woman.

The royal princess who drew the baby out of the river immediately intuits that an Israelite mother is trying to save her son through Miriam. The narrative inverts Pharaoh's decree of male infant extermination when his own daughter permits Miriam to provide the child with his own mother. In order for the mother and sister to resist their circumstances, they intentionally engage in what is necessary rather than to passively experience what their circumstances determine to be their fate. There are no discussions, no meetings; there is only the time to engage with purpose. It is Miriam's skill as a leader that transforms the Nile River from a place of death into the source of her brother's name, Moses—drawn from the water. An older sister determines the destiny of her brother, who will be called to lead the people out of their suffering.

Miriam, Aaron, and Moses are unique among siblings in the Bible. Each of them is linked to the redemption of the Israelites and the experience of revelation at Sinai and finally the wanderings. The Exodus, or redemption of Israel, required both Moses and Aaron to facilitate the ten plagues that finally led to the people's freedom. Miriam and Moses both sang on the other side of the Sea of Reeds. Miriam and Aaron witnessed the unique experience of Sinai at which the people were given the laws and teachings that defined their destiny. Each is textually described as absolutely essential to the narrative, yet each as a complex human is missing something. In the end, Moses, Miriam, and Aaron all lack the element of Israel—the people and land of Israel. None of them entered the land to which they led the people. Moses, Miriam, and Aaron are . . . incomplete—imperfect.

Miriam does not appear again in the biblical text until after the Exodus from Egypt when Moses and the people have had the "miraculous" experience at the *Yam Suf*, the Sea of Reeds (Exod 15:20-21). Exodus 15, one of the oldest texts in the Torah, is a lyric poem or song. It recounts the songs of praise sung by the Israelites to mark their freedom. "Then Moses and the Israelites sang this song to the Lord . . . " (Exod 15:1), which is parallel to "Then Miriam the prophetess, Aaron's sister, took a timbral in her hand, and all the women went out after her in dance with timbrals. And Miriam chanted for them . . . " (Exod 15:20-21). These ancient songs with warrior images glorify the Unseeable God who saves Israel from slavery and then from destruction by Pharaoh's army.

Moses and Miriam take it upon themselves to sing and dance, to celebrate the miraculous distortions of nature and the slaughter of so many Egyptians. This celebration of gratitude seems a bit strange if not inappropriate way to express our universal view of humanity. When the "Messengers on High" join in the singing, a rabbinic teaching claims that God chastised them for ignoring that "the Egyptians are my children, too." This moral rebuke became a custom during the annual Passover Seder. We remove ten drops of wine from our glasses to reduce our joy in memory of the ten plagues.

Miriam's unique role in leading the women in song and dance concerns some of the rabbis who fear that she might have been challenging Moses. More contemporary thinkers remind us that celebration is a unique form of confrontation and resistance. Miriam is a reminder of the teaching of the rabbinic sages, that when the Messianic Age begins, all the biblical sacrifices will be nullified, except the thanksgiving sacrifice, because one should never stop saying thank you. Miriam takes charge of leading the community in singing and dancing, so they can physically experience the gratitude of the inexplicable redemption.

Miriam is absent from the experience of Sinai and the wilderness, until Numbers 12. Here we read that she and Aaron spoke against Moses because he married a "Cushite woman." They also publicly challenged him, "Has the Eternal spoken only through Moses? Has God not spoken through us as well?" (Num 12:1-2) For these outspoken communal statements, God punishes only Miriam with "snow-white scales" and being forced outside the camp for seven days. Aaron, the High Priest, who also challenged Moses, is not punished and Moses prays to God for Miriam's healing.

Rabbinic interpreters attempted, centuries later, to explain and interpret this one example of conflict between the sibling leaders. Most argue that Moses was not marrying a different woman, a second wife, but recommitting himself to Zipporah, the wife we met in Exodus 3. Moses had given himself over to the all-consuming needs of both God and the people and had not been present as a husband or father. Miriam spoke out in support of Zipporah and that the leader had fundamental responsibilities to his family that had been neglected. Moses has argued he must always be separate, ready for God's presence, and therefore cannot be with his family. Miriam argues that even a leader of God's nation can be a man who cares for the building block of that nation, the family.

Miriam has no husband nor child in the biblical text, yet she is punished for arguing on behalf of the absent Zipporah. The rabbis are sensitive to Miriam's "singleness" so they retroactively assign her an important husband, Hur, and son, Caleb. This also puts her in the genealogical line of King David. Though textually she is a strong independent woman, the rabbinic tradition wants her to meet their standards of wife and mother. She is punished for speaking out with her independence, and then the text reminds us that even strong women during this time could only be healed by men, in this case, her younger brother. The biblical text offers us a model of a single independent woman limited by the ancient context of a male-dominated world.

Miriam's presence in such an ancient text continues to remind us about the still necessary work of protecting women who are tragically ignored. I often thought about Miriam during the years I worked in India with HIV/AIDS prevention and orphan care. Far too many times, the clinic doctor asked my help to explain to a woman that her husband who had just died had a disease that he had probably transmitted to her. These women were widows with children in rural India who had lost their identity and in that social system were now considered worthless.

In one case, two children were left in a village hut where their mother had died. Their grandmother brought them to the clinic. Another two children were found sitting next to their mother's body in a train station. AIDS orphans in India are often created when a father contracts the virus from sex workers, infects their mother, who then infects her children through pregnancy. Then the mother is rejected by both families and the general society. India remains an extreme example of women whose autonomy is denied to them in life and who, when they are infected, are often exiled to die alone.

I often spoke of Miriam's strong biblical presence as a single woman to AIDS widows where single women are not a traditional model of hope. Young widows in the HIV/AIDS pandemic are particularly vulnerable to stigma and marginalization. Organizations like the UN must continue to educate global communities where women continue to be ignored.

Contemporary studies of women in various leadership roles reveal that all women face similar cultural biases. All too often, those hiring or promoting women assume that they need time to be mothers, which makes employers less likely to offer women additional responsibility or larger roles. Though it is illegal to ask a woman about children, most studies suggest an inherent bias in every profession. A recent study found that the majority of men in Germany and Japan were still against women accepting leadership roles that in any way compromised their roles as mothers.

Stereotypic traits of strong women, such as sensitivity and concern for others, are often experienced as negatives when leaders are chosen. This bias against feminine characteristics distorts the selection process in business, politics, and academia. In instances where men continue to dominate the process, leadership roles are given to individuals who seem more like those choosing or those currently in the executive positions. Women pushing for other women are worried that their objectivity will be questioned. Several studies have concluded that the tensions between men and women reflect barriers that women face at play, at work, at home, and in their various communities.

The biblical texts that illuminate Miriam confirm that these same tensions were also part of her ancient culture. The enigmatic episode regarding Miriam's outspoken challenge about Moses concludes, ". . . and the people did not march until Miriam was readmitted" (Num 12:15). The people supported her, softening the image of sibling conflict, but then she vanishes from the text again. Until Num 20:1 concludes with the unexpected and unexplained statement: "Miriam died there and was buried there." This is Miriam, the older sister and prophetess who saved Moses and later sang and danced after the now freed slaves crossed the sea. She dies without even being given an age.

Aaron, her younger brother, who assisted Moses during the plagues and became the first High Priest, also dies at the very end of this chapter, Num 20:24-29. His death is directly related to one final confrontation with the people, thirst, and a divine source of water. The biblical text offers explanations and testimonials, that Aaron dies, ". . . in the sight of the whole community" (vs. 27b) and ". . . all the house of Israel bewailed Aaron for thirty days" (vs. 29b).

This last description of communal mourning is the source of Jewish tradition's custom, *Shaloshim*, the first thirty days of grief.

The biblical text of Miriam's death is a half verse that indicates only that she was alone. This unexpected and stark ending for Miriam must have upset rabbinic commentators. They interpret that the people rebel again without water because with Miriam's absence the miraculous freshwater spring that followed her in the wilderness vanishes. This fresh water well, created by God, according to the rabbis, was a rock full of holes that flows with water. This rabbinic explanation requires the reader's willingness to recognize the two consecutive passages and accept an interpretation that intentionally repairs Miriam's image. The rabbis link Miriam to water to teach us that she was a source of vitality, a unique leader who cared for the people's needs in the wilderness.

During the many years of teaching the Hebrew Bible at a state university, I have used this chapter of Scripture to illustrate that, in my view, this ancient text is inherently sexist. Miriam is essential for the narrative about Moses. She is defiant and independent, not defined by her relationship to a husband or son. Her participation in the actual experience of redemption is unique. She leads the women in song and dance. She makes sure that *all the people* who are freed are given an opportunity to express their gratitude, not just the men! Then she is absent until she and Aaron challenge their brother's personal family decisions, for which she alone is punished. Finally, she dies, alone, in the wilderness, as if she had never been there.

Miriam's presence on the riverbank assured the survival of an Israelite infant whose existence had been prohibited by the Pharaoh. Again, Miriam is present on the other side of the *Yam Suf,* the Sea of Reeds, to lead the people in an act of unique celebration. When we find Miriam near the water, she is a strong woman, leading the people in her own way toward their freedom. She saves their eventual leader and teaches them how to thank God with joy. Her leadership is not directed by God nor her brothers. Miriam is like the life-sustaining water her presence provides. She is simply there, among the people, textually absent, her life undeveloped and seemingly empty. She dies without age or explanation, her life of leadership taken for granted.

The Hebrew Bible as an ancient text cannot be evaluated by our contemporary egalitarian standards. Yet 3500 years after Miriam, women still only earn 80 percent of the salary offered to men in the same position with the same qualifications. The rights for women to determine their own reproduction decisions continue to be determined primarily by men who remain dominant in legislatures and courts. Though women remain at the very core of life's mysteries, they are still ignored. Women, like Miriam, essential to every human narrative, still aren't communally as recognized as men.

The contemporary increase of religious extremes among Jews, Christians, and Muslims has once again destabilized the stature of women even as they have marked significant historical progress. Consider the tragic cultures that prohibit the education of girls. Young girls who are raised with fear and taught to be submissive even as we continue to fight for the basic human rights of literacy and economic autonomy for all women. Women still do not have equal access to professional education in many twenty-first-century countries. Extremist religious communities still do not treat women equally, denying them the right to lead worship, study of Scripture and, of course, from being ordained.

Women today are not as ignored as Miriam in her death, but neither are they celebrated for their many gifts of leadership. Full gender equality will take much more time and effort, even as we celebrate the progress we have achieved. It is simply too easy to take women for granted because their very presence sustains us as much as the water we must have to live. We have not yet learned how to share power or the many burdens we all face in our complex world. Miriam teaches us that though the strongest of women in the biblical text were incomplete, thinking about them today reminds us that our differences in gender cannot become our "missing piece."

6

Moses: The Good-Enough Leader

The figure that dominates the Torah, the first five books of the Hebrew Bible, is Moses. From the outset of Exodus to the last verse in Deuteronomy, he is the leader, prophet, lawgiver, judge, and mediator that takes one generation of slaves out of Egypt and leads the next generation of Israelites to their Promised Land. Moses is held up as one of the greatest leaders of all time—an example for all kinds of leaders today. The Hebrew Bible declares without equivocation: "Never again did there arise in Israel a prophet like Moses— whom the Lord singled out face to face" (Deut 34:10). The biblical text claims that Moses was the best model of leadership.

The classic theory of leadership, the "great man," is the driving force of history, not simply a product of his surroundings. The Bible portrays Moses as the man who shaped the history of the Israelites' freedom from slavery. Winston Churchill, surely one of the greatest leaders of the twentieth century, wrote about Moses in 1932, *Moses: The Leader of a People*: ". . . *in identifying one of the greatest of human beings with the most decisive leap forward ever discernible in the human story.*"[1] Freud used Moses as a way to explain his personal rejection of his father's Judaism. Michelangelo's unique marble statue of Moses is considered one of the greatest pieces of art in human history. Literature and cinema have left their own images of this man whose presence as a unique leader cannot be diminished by questions about the historical facticity

1. Gilbert, *Churchill and the Jews*, 95.

of the Bible's accounts of his life. In other words, Moses the leader has been integrated into many dimensions of Western culture as a unique and powerful figure.

The biblical text describes Moses as someone whose greatness is imperfect, that he is missing one essential element that defines Jewish life—he is denied the right to enter into the land of Israel with the freed people of Israel. The Bible presents Moses as a multi-dimensional human being. If Moses remains a model for leaders in today's world, it is because he is fully human. It is his shared humanity that makes him accessible, even though we only read about him in the ancient biblical texts. If the biblical Moses is a model for today, then let us engage him with the same issues that challenge us.

Among our most stressful life struggles is our integration of change, especially the rapid change of technology. Although we have only had smartphones for ten years, some are already certain that the iPhone can be compared to Gutenberg's printing press—considered the single most important device for the creation of communal literacy. In 2018, 253 million Americans spent up to 370 billion waking hours and $349 billion just on their smartphones. These statistics are further illuminated by a university study which found similarities between use of smartphones and substance abuse. The consensus of research on screen time reveals its addictive properties: screen time triggers a dopamine response in our brains, and when we are deprived of screen time, we feel anxious.

The changes produced by science and technology continue to distort our understanding of time. Astronomers teach that the universe is 13.8 billion years old, with all of human history taking place in just the last 300,000 years. We recently saw the first ever computerized images of a Black Hole. The image, recorded by radio telescopes, is of an event that took place 55 million years ago and is still occurring, a fact which astronomers and physicists will confirm but cannot explain. This kind of global experience has distorted our perspective of history, making it possible to compare the smartphone technology of 2008 to the 1440 invention of the printing press.

A noted contemporary social critic and journalist, Tom Friedman, wrote that we have been "dislocated" by so much change in such a short time, and people simply cannot keep up. We have had to accept so much technological change that we're now experiencing a "cultural angst" because we are aware that no individual can ever learn *everything* there is to know. Medical research confirms this new "toxic stress" and its unique anxiety that impacts especially those who lead us in every aspect of life. The World Health Organization points to the increased depression among young adults. A global mental health study concludes that there has been a significant increase in "perfectionism" among especially those attending university and college.

This "dislocation" motivated Rabbi Levi Weiman-Kelman to prepare the congregation he founded before every worship service. I watched him stand quietly and have everyone close their eyes, take a deep breath, and quietly sing a simple chant in Hebrew from Psalms. I heard him teach people everywhere he went to use their silence, breath, and simple music as serious elements of worship. Over the years he modeled how this simple technique provides worshipers with an opportunity to "locate" themselves, shutting out the angst of dislocation and the daily burden of polarizing change.

Moses too faces an experience of "dislocation" when he learns that he is an Israelite. The biblical text offers no explanation of how he learns this or how much time he took to accept the "truth" (Exod 2:11). We can only imagine how a very young, immature Moses came to grips with this secret. When he understands his actual heritage, he chooses to experience life among the enslaved Israelites and witnesses their oppression. He sees an Egyptian beat an Israelite and now Moses must confront the violence as an attack on *his* community.

The text states that Moses "turns this way and that" and seeing no one, strikes (kills) the Egyptian, and buries him. In this first textual encounter with Moses since his infancy, the biblical text provides descriptions of fear, decisiveness, and an intentional rejection of his adopted Egyptian identity. Moses is engaged in *his* community, responding to ruthless injustice and persecution.

One cannot find this essential biblical experience included in any of the articles or essays depicting Moses as an ideal leader. I cannot imagine praising leaders who "make a killing"—an idiom for a big success—or training them to "take no prisoner" and not let anyone get in your way by using Moses' act of violence. And yet, this act of violence was a pivotal part of Moses' path to leadership. He is imperfect, just like we are. Afraid he will be caught, Moses flees Egypt and becomes a shepherd.

Being a shepherd requires a total commitment of time and learning to experience the animals' needs. It is during Moses' work as a shepherd that he meets his wife and finds a mentor in her father. Being human means that we learn our most important life lessons from the struggles we all face in actual life-experiences. Thus Moses, the still developing leader, must have learned some essential skills in his own life experiences. Finally, it is his behavior as a shepherd that brings him into an encounter with God.

Moses encounters Abraham's God in fire that burns but miraculously does not consume a bush. Moses acknowledges his extraordinary experience by looking away in awe and surprise. In response, God discloses the Divine presence in confirmation of Moses' unique human awareness. The rabbis imagine God thinking: "If this is how he cares for the sheep of man, he is definitely fit to shepherd Mine . . ."[2]

Unlike his first experience among the enslaved Israelites, Moses seems less impulsive, completely engaged by the miraculous experience. Moses does not doubt nor argue about the reality he experiences of God in the mystery bush. Unexpectedly, he finds himself in a job interview. Moses tries to argue that he is unfit for the position and that, as a stammering speaker, he will be an unconvincing representative of Divine intervention. Suddenly, he is a reluctant leader who requires the extraordinary

2. "*Midrash Rabbah, Shemot Rabbah 2:2*"

power of a rod to convince both the Israelites and Pharaoh that he really does represent God.

Too often we study leaders and their skills, forgetting that there was a period *before* they were great. Moses kills an Egyptian, finds God in a foreign land, and accepts a call to lead the Israelites out of slavery, but at what point in this narrative does he become the leader? The ten plagues, actual Exodus from Egypt, and crossing the Sea of Reeds are all Divine acts in which Moses is present but not leading. The people are transformed by the events, but we know nothing about how these events transformed Moses as a leader.

Immediately following the celebration of gratitude after crossing the Sea of Reeds, the now freed slaves experience life on their own; they feel hunger and thirst. Exodus 16 and 17 indicate that getting to the Promised Land will not be as easy as some imagined. The people constantly complain to Moses about their thirst and hunger, even though God does provide for them through their leader. Moses receives his only leadership training in Exodus 18 when Yitro, his father-in-law, explains that he cannot possibly serve all the people's needs; he must delegate some of these responsibilities. Moses appoints seventy elders, but more importantly, it is the only time we find Moses aware that he cannot do it all. Being the perfect leader for both this people and God is not possible.

It is too bad that Moses, the still-in-training-one-time-only leader of biblical freed slaves, did not have the opportunity to study the writings of D. W. Winnicott.[3] The mid-twentieth century British pediatrician and psychoanalyst studied infants and their mothers. Winnicott concluded that children needed parents who were "good enough" and not perfect. The child must also learn how to cope with anger and disappointment. The studies show that even infants are learning about resilience as they experience the outside world. Winnicott wanted parents to learn that their children cannot possibly have their every need satisfied, and that both the parents and children will be okay. This public lesson in 1953 was liberating for new parents facing a still difficult life in post-war England.

3. Ades, "Winnicott."

Being a good enough parent, doctor, teacher, or leader is not about mediocrity, but about the real-life choices we all must make in response to the limits in our lives. It is an insight of modernity that perfection is neither a realistic nor ideal goal. Parents naturally want to be perfect but must also engage in their own adult world. Winnicott taught that spending a lifetime trying to be a perfect mother hurts the child's development and will ultimately destroy the mother's sense of self. Every parent is obligated to teach their child not to neglect their own needs, and that taking care of yourself is not selfish, but a necessary commitment to survival. Moses needed to learn that being a good enough leader would have been acceptable.

No one taught Moses that he and the people he was leading were imperfect. There could be no expectation of perfection because there is no such reality. Moses would have benefitted from Winnicott's studies: parents are raising human children in an imperfect world where disappointment, anger, frustration, and unfairness are realities that everyone must confront. Moses cannot lead and raise these child-like freed slaves into an independent people unless he himself is permitted to be less than perfect.

Exodus 32 introduces the reader to an entirely new Moses, one who has spent forty days and nights on top of Mt. Sinai, engaged with the Unseen and Unseeable Unique God. The text says simply, that "the people saw that Moses was so long/delayed in coming down," and they rebelled. The people had changed radically from suffering slaves into a worshipping community, receiving the Torah at Mt. Sinai. Imagine the stress from these changes: they were beaten, starved and persecuted, cried out and experienced the signs and wonders of the Exodus, and then the mystery of Divine revelation. Moses was late because he was with God, but the people could not wait and they needed immediate satisfaction, so they turned to an idol and pagan worship. Maybe it was the stress of so much change that caused their panic, fear, and impatience.

Moses is late and Miriam is absent, so Aaron responds to the people's panic and needs. They are afraid that Moses won't return. Their religious identities are immature, and they want a physical experience of belief. The people don't realize that God is engaging their needs when Moses is commanded to build a tabernacle with an Ark to hold the Divine tablets. The people's need for immediate gratification prevents them from appreciating that God too wants them to have a physical focus, hence the Ark of the Tabernacle.

God warns Moses, "Hurry down, for *your* people, whom *you* brought out of the land of Egypt, have acted basely . . . " (Exod 32:7). The italicized words are Divine sarcasm. The people who now worship idols belong to you, Moses. I—*God*—am done with them! Moses responds with a deftly persuasive leadership style. Did you bring the Israelites here to destroy them? Moses selflessly defends the people and leaves the mountain top with the Divinely inscribed tablets.

As he came down the mountain he was probably distracted about Aaron, Miriam, Jethro, and the seventy elders, none of whom seemed to take any responsibility. Aaron, the priest, is responsible for all worship. How could he have let them make an idol? Miriam celebrated and sang on the other side of the Sea. Where was she? By any reasonable standards, the Golden Calf is a failure of leadership, yet only Moses seems to be the one who is accountable. Moses knows about the idol and hears the singing, but the dancing enrages him because of memories of the same people singing and dancing in gratitude to God after they crossed the Sea of Reeds.

On top of the mountain, he decisively defends the people, but something happened when he comes down and witnesses their celebration in front of the idol. The leader who served both God and the people destroys the Divine tablets when he experiences the unique stress of being accountable to both God and the people he leads. Smashing those tablets was a combination of decisive leadership, impulsive human anger, and emotional exhaustion. Leaders whose roles and responsibilities have been completely transformed need training. The shepherd's initial encounter has become a daily mix of politics, religion, military tactics, and always being the people's advocate. Poor Moses. Someone should have told him that all we really need is for you to be a good enough leader!

I never got any training on being a prison chaplain, but to my surprise I learned how to serve men in a maximum-security state penitentiary by listening. The Indiana State Prison in Michigan City was physically imposing on the outside, and on the inside it was a life-changing experience. I received a call from the warden explaining that he had heard I was the new rabbi in Michigan City, and he hoped that I could meet the Jews in the prison. I had not heard anything about Jews in the state prison during my interview at Sinai Temple nor since moving to town, but I said yes. A week later, I entered the prison gates for the first time without any expectations or preparations. The warden met me, shook my hand, and gave me files on the four men I would meet. I walked through four different sliding gates with armed guards inside control booths. The sound of a prison gate closing is unique, and I looked around realizing that I was inside a small area with three rooms and no windows.

I met the four men, listened to their stories, and answered their questions. Two of the men were Jews and wanted me to help the other two men study about Judaism. They were all incarcerated for violent crimes, but they seemed friendly and respectful. This first visit was the start of a series of regular visits, and the group changed as the population of the prison changed. At one time there were eleven men who came to worship, study, and seek my pastoral counseling. We learned from each other about being a responsible person before we could repent and be accepted again in the community. They taught me that anyone in the wrong circumstances has the potential of committing a terrible crime, but that there are some people who choose to embrace criminal behavior more than others.

One visit remains forever in my mind and heart. The inmates received our congregational bulletin as a newsletter and had read that one of our Torah scrolls could not be repaired and was to be buried. I taught them that a Sefer Torah had God's name written and the scroll had been created for sacred use but was now *Pa'sul* (unfit) and would be buried in the Jewish cemetery. They all listened and then asked me if they could write a letter to the congregation asking if they could use this *Pa'sul* Torah because they were *Pa'sul* Jews. Their question surprised me and moved me to tears.

They wrote a letter to the Board of Trustees explaining that they wanted the Torah to confirm that they were really a synagogue. They had begun to build an Ark that would be kept in the Catholic Chapel behind locked doors. The leaders of my congregation were surprised that I had been spending so much time in the prison and some were upset that I had encouraged the men to write the letter. It took a few meetings with individuals and a second meeting with the group for me to convince them that these prisoners all understood their sins and the shame they brought to themselves, their families, and the Jewish community. I taught my leaders that these men saw themselves as unfit/*Pa'sul*. We did not need to make it worse by telling these Jews, "You are so unfit we would rather bury our Torah than have you use it." Just enough people supported the prisoners' request, but some people never talked to me about my prison work again. Sometimes the best you can be is just good enough.

The Moses of the book of Numbers is not the same person we knew in Exodus. The people continued to challenge him with their hunger and thirst, always complaining nostalgically about their lives in Egypt. Numbers 20 begins: "The Israelites arrived in a group at the wilderness of Zin on the first new moon and the people stayed at Kadesh." One commentary notes that this is only two years into their wandering with thirty-eight years remaining. Moses' sister dies and immediately the people challenge him again about their thirst. They have not stopped complaining, even though he has continued to defend them. Leaders must care about themselves and model to their community how to stop, grieve, and respect their own family. But there is nothing in the text to suggest that Moses did anything to care for himself after his sister died.

God tells Moses and Aaron to command the rock and water will pour out to satisfy the people's contentious mood. In Exodus 17, God had instructed him to take the rod and strike the rock, but in Numbers 20, Moses is instructed only to speak to the rock. The people are rebelling, and have not matured with resilience, patience, or perspective. Moses is told to speak to the rock, but he strikes the rock. Maybe his grief confuses him with the earlier experience, or he is exhausted and angry with the people. The text does not provide any details about time or intention. It simply states that he struck the rock a second time, and it was this act that defied God. Rabbinic commentators say that the first strike was passion but the second was intentional. Moses knew what he was doing in front of the people.

In that instant, there is a convergence—Miriam's death, the people's unending demands, and Moses' exhaustion interwoven with the toxic stress of all the changes he had experienced. Maybe it was his realization of still another thirty-eight years with this same people and God's demands, an impossible balance. Regardless of the explanations, he intentionally defies both the source of his authority and the purpose of his leadership. I think that he was always a human who cared profoundly for God and the people. Tragically he didn't stop to care for himself as he cared for God and the people. He lacked reassurance that being an imperfect human was all anyone expected; he was a good enough prophet and leader.

His legacy is being the only prophet to know God face to face and being unable to show that trust for God in public. Our greatest strengths are also our greatest weakness. Moses always wanted to know God intimately, so he accepted the role as the leader God needed. But not even Moses could stay on top of the mountain *and* calm the people at the same time before they built an idol. There were no previous models to study nor any training to help either Moses or God. No one can be everything to everybody. Moses learned again and again, no one can have it all.

Moses represents an ideal that must continue to be debated, analyzed, and deconstructed by every generation. Evaluating leaders requires determining their whole lives, including their personal lives as life-partners and as parents. The only thing we know for certain about Moses' personal life is its absence in the text. Moses can only be evaluated on his work, on his willingness to serve the people and defend them, no matter their behavior. No leader today would accept the roles and responsibilities of Moses as defined by insatiability of the people and God as it was described in the biblical text. Today, we must resist perfectionism and its risks of depression and isolation. Moses was one of a kind; someone to be understood not imitated.

7

David: Naked Power

We are living in a time of reckoning for those who have abused their power. Women have come forward and publicly challenged icons of male power for decades of serial sexual abuse. Men of exceptional talent and international renown have been professionally held accountable. Still others have been criminally charged and convicted for intentionally hurting women, sometimes even teenagers, under the care of coaches and trainers. These were truly brazen acts, without any shame, blatant demands of entitlement.

Another example is the brazen manipulation of the cost of pharmaceuticals and the shameless greed of these businesses. Illness is global with ongoing pandemics or the threat that a local outbreak could become global. The price of medicine has little relation to the cost of its development or production, and there is such global diversity of prices that people purchase drugs from online stores that provide hundreds, even thousands, of dollars of discounts.

We are living with the global HIV/AIDS pandemic, without a vaccine nor a cure, and the drugs required for even basic antiviral treatment remain so costly that millions of people remain untreated. Multinational companies have the naked power to increase the price of a drug used for AIDS patients, from $13.50 a pill to $750. This arbitrary increase has cost thousands of lives. Brazil demanded that her citizens had the right to medications regardless of the legal boundaries of patents, and so since 1988 generic drugs have been produced without regard of intellectual property rights. But these sorts of actions are few and far between.

I served on the Presidential Advisory Council for HIV/AIDS under the administration of Bill Clinton. I challenged a leading medical expert about governmental funded research and private corporate profits. I learned from my experience on the Advisory Council about power being exercised without regard for ethics or the needs of the most vulnerable people.

Clinton's council had studied the impact of clean needle exchange and the transmission of the HIV virus. Scientists concluded that intervening by providing clean needles would diminish the transmission of the virus. The council studied, discussed, and voted that the President should exercise his power to permit clean needle exchange in Federal prisons and support state and local programs of clean needle exchange. But this was a political risk for the president because most of the country (and most of Congress) would not approve of government funds being used to support IV drug use, even if it prevented the transmission of the HIV virus.

The President accepted and, we thought, approved of our findings. But then, after a long conversation with his "drug-czar" returning from South America, the president changed his mind—opting to prioritize political concerns and his image in Congress. Several members of the council threatened to resign in letters of protest. I gave a sermon equating President Clinton's decision to FDR's decision not to bomb concentration camps in Europe after learning their purpose. I sent the sermon to members of the Presidential Council and it was passed to the president. A few years after he retired, Clinton made a statement at a global AIDS meeting admitting his political error and failure to follow the findings of his own council. He has said that people in need had been sacrificed to the power of the politics.

These and other examples of the brazen abuse of power, whether for greed or a sense of entitlement, share a shameless intentionality. This curious idiom, "shameless," immediately links us to the Hebrew Bible. The verse Gen 2:25 challenges us directly: "The two of them were naked . . . yet they felt no shame." Usually, we read this simply as a description of Adam and Eve's innocence prior to eating from the Tree of Moral Knowledge. These first two humans did not yet have the knowledge to discern between right and wrong, thus being naked meant nothing to them.

The text provokes us with an enigmatic double-negative— "*not*" being ashamed. In the next verse we immediately meet the serpent, who in a Hebrew pun is also described as "*Arum*," which sounds like naked but actually means cunning. Is the text providing us an ancient comparison of the first humans who were simply naked and without shame with the snake whose intentional manipulation was shameless?

Being nude does not stimulate "shame" until the humans intentionally eat from the Tree of Moral Knowledge. Their choices created shadows of shame because of their new awareness of moral judgement. Once your choice casts shadows of right and wrong, then being naked loses its innocence. Once being human includes the critical self-awareness of right and wrong, the text tells us that they become "afraid" of being naked (Gen 3:10).

It was the serpent whose shamelessness connected these first humans to moral awareness. Never again can a human be innocent of this basic sense of communal moral judgement. We cannot pretend that we are unashamed when we intentionally uncover our naked desires for power. Today, far too many of the intentional acts of abusive power in business, politics, or human rights are meant to be brazen, shameless. What we might call the abuse of "naked power."

The excesses of naked power displayed by one biblical figure, King David, continue to challenge us. He is the biblical figure mentioned more than any other in the Hebrew Bible. His spiritual charisma and passion ignite Jewish identity even today. David is the second King in the history of Israel, and father of Solomon; he united the tribes and conquered the most biblical land. Tradition claims he is the author of the book of Psalms, and biblical genealogies trace the Messiah through David's family. Western culture and history have inflated this biblical character through art and literature. The fifteen-year-old biblical shepherd/

warrior, David, was immortalized in 1504 in the fourteen-foot marble sculpture by Michelangelo, considered to be one of the greatest pieces of art ever created.

The Star of David, a symbol of Jewish destiny, is comprised of two triangles overlapping into a six-pointed star. This symbol was found as early as fourth-century CE on an arch of an ancient synagogue in the Galilee. The star's use among Jews as a communal symbol became normative in the fourteenth century CE in Central Europe, and it became the official symbol of Zionism in 1897. The Nazis twisted it into their yellow ID badge inside of which was the word "Jew" in every European language under Nazi control. After centuries, David the biblical King is permanently synthesized into the Star of David, which everyone recognizes on the flag of Israel and the universal symbol of both Jews and Judaism.

Like Abraham and Moses, David also has only two of the three defining characteristics of Jewish life. David has Israel, in both land and people. Through Nathan, the prophet, the King engages the ethical dynamics of Torah. David offers to construct the Temple but is told by Nathan that God will establish David's offspring on the throne and that he will build "a house for My name" (2 Sam 7:13). Inevitably, David is missing God because he is not permitted to build the Temple in Jerusalem. Moses is denied the right to enter the Promised Land with the people of Israel, the very goal of his mission. He is punished for his public lack of trust in God. David, a hero, King, and spiritual author yearns to be the builder of God's throne on earth, but he too is denied his most passionate desire. Like Moses, he is punished for his behavior; David lacks God because ultimately, he has "blood on his hands."

The text that narrates David's unique naked power, his affair with Bathsheba, is 2 Samuel 11–12. The biblical text has a terse brevity that prompts endless questions. It begins when wars are fought and kings go out, yet David "remained in Jerusalem . . . and late one afternoon, he strolls on his roof." Here is a man with so much power that while others are in battle, he can "stroll" on his roof and happen to see a very beautiful woman bathing.

David sends someone to "inquire about her," and he is informed of both Bathsheba's father, Eliam and of her husband, Uriah. The King of Israel now knows both her tribal identity and that she is married, which according to biblical law makes her forbidden to anyone else. The text makes sure that the reader is aware of the boundaries that should limit even the power of the King.

"David sent messengers to *fetch her*; she came to him *and he lay with her*—she had just purified herself after her period—and she went back home" (2 Sam 11:4, *emphasis mine).* David ignores her status, impersonally sends messengers to *fetch/take* her and she comes to the palace. He uses his power to *lay with her*—inappropriate sexual contact that many today would define as rape. David, the King, saw someone he wanted and exercised his naked power, and then sent her home! The text signals the reader of one simple human reality: she has just been "purified" after her monthly menstrual cycle; she is fertile!

There is no textual evidence that Bathsheba was attempting to seduce the King. David has a harem of concubines to choose from, yet he decides to inappropriately and forcibly engage sexually with a married woman whose husband is one of his warriors. Rabbinic commentaries attempt to protect both David and Bathsheba because their son is King Solomon, and the Sages do not want to stain him with a moral judgement.

The #MeToo movement has globally transformed how we read, understand, and discuss the behavior of men in power. Powerful men have, in the past, been able to keep silent the women whom they have harassed, assaulted, and raped. These victims are now expressing themselves, and so we cannot engage in this text and ignore Bathsheba. The brevity and ambiguity of the biblical text leaves doubts about whether this was a consensual relationship. The biblical text does not offer Bathsheba a voice; we learn nothing from her point of view.

Geraldine Brooks, a contemporary author, provides Bathsheba's absent voice in *The Secret Chord: A Novel*. In the book, Bathsheba painfully erases the ambiguity of the text. She corrects the prophet Nathan's assumptions: "Do you have any idea what he was like that night? He used me like some—receptacle. The bruises on my breasts took a month to fade. I was afraid Uriah would come on leave and see the marks. . . . When he bundled me out—tossing me a jewel, as if I were a whore requiring payment—it was over for him, but not for me." Only then must Nathan, the prophet, admit, ". . . he had been raping her, and I had let myself call it a seduction."[1]

The actual biblical narrative continues when Bathsheba sends a messenger to inform David that she is pregnant. David immediately sends for her husband Uriah, who is fighting on behalf of the King. Now David becomes calculating. He has to cover up the adultery and pregnancy. The text relates the King's almost comedic attempts to lure the good solider, Uriah, to spend just enough time with his wife to create the credible doubt of paternity. Uriah is portrayed as being more ethical than the King; he is not tempted even by royal wine to enjoy his conjugal rights.

After David's charade fails, he reverts to his naked power and sends Uriah back into battle. "In the morning, David wrote a letter to Joab, which he sent with Uriah" (2 Sam 11:14). The King orders his general to place Uriah in harm's way and shamelessly has Uriah deliver his own "death-sentence"! King David, heroic warrior, author of the Psalms, and beloved of God, who ultimately provides the

---

1. Brooks, *The Secret Chord*, 231-232.

royal genealogy of the Messianic ruler. This same man uses battle to murder the husband of the woman he adulterously impregnated. It is a scene that one might expect in *The Godfather*.

Bathsheba hears of her husband's death and laments for him. After mourning seven days, David brings her to the palace where she "becomes his wife and bore him a son" (vs. 27b). This is the only contact David and Bathsheba have since the night of their adultery. The next chapter immediately begins with, "But the Lord was displeased with what David had done . . ." God's judgement comes only after Uriah is dead and a baby is to be born, which is announced by Nathan the prophet's divine chastisement.

Nathan uses a parable—a rhetorical tool that teaches through analogy. David is portrayed as being clueless which further engages the reader who understands from the outset what Nathan is doing. "There are two men in the same city, one rich and one poor. The rich man had very large flocks and herds, but the poor man had only one little ewe lamb that he had bought. He tended it and it grew up together with him and his children; it used to share his morsel of bread, drink from his cup and nestle in his bosom; it was like a daughter to him. One day, a traveler came to the rich man, but he was loath to take anything from his own flocks or herds to prepare a meal for the guest who had come to him, so he took the poor man's lamb and prepared it for the man who had come to him. David flew into a rage against the man . . ." (2 Sam 12:1-5a).

Nathan stimulates David's sense of justice; the issues of right and wrong are obvious. David, the righteous King, easily indicts the man who had everything. ". . . the man who did this deserves to die! He shall pay for the lamb four times over, because he showed not pity" (12:5b–6). Now Nathan slaps David with the sting of reality: "You are that man!" Of course, the reader is not shocked, and neither is David. "I stand guilty before the Lord!" And Nathan replies to David, "The Lord has remitted your sin; you shall not die."

Nathan declares to David his immediate punishment: ". . . the child about to be born to you shall die" (12:13–14). The infant becomes critically ill, remains unnamed, and dies within seven days. After the child's death, David immediately returns to his normal life.

"David consoled his wife Bathsheba; he went to her and lay with her. She bore a son and she named him Solomon" (12:24). The text underscores the importance of the House of David with the birth of Solomon without any reference to any of the scandal.

To David's credit and legacy, he expresses contrition through Psalm 51, a confession and prayer of repentance: "I recognize my transgressions and am ever conscious of my sin" (Ps 51:5). Like the first humans who had no shame prior to gaining moral knowledge but became afraid in God's presence after they learned the difference between right and wrong, David too is afraid. "You are just in in Your sentence, and right in Your judgment. . . . Do not cast me out of Your presence or take Your holy spirit away from me" (Ps 51:6a, 13). The David we hear in the Psalms has none of the arrogant entitlement of the Bathsheba narrative.

David is mentioned more than any other figure in the Hebrew Bible. He is a hero, beloved warrior and King who establishes Jerusalem as the ancient capital. Textually, he is the father of King Solomon whose wisdom produces Proverbs, Ecclesiastes, and the Song of Songs. David becomes the anchor of the Messianic promise as expressed in the Gospels. Finally, in one of the latest texts of the Hebrew Bible, we find the strongest statement of David's accountability.

In 1 Chr 22:7-8, David explains to Solomon that "the word of the Lord came to me saying . . . You have shed much blood . . . for you shed much blood on the earth in my sight." Here God explains directly to David without the prophet Nathan. The text includes the King's "great battles" but emphasizes twice the shedding of much blood. I think this refers to David's responsibility for the murders of Uriah and the unnamed son born of Uriah's wife. David "shed much blood . . . in My sight." David's acts were brazen and without shame; hence God says without equivocation, "You shall not build a House for My Name."

These later moments of accountability in the book of Psalms and Chronicles sustain the honor of King David. Like all other great biblical figures, David cannot have it all; he is denied what he wants: to build God's House. He cannot claim that he, King David, brought God to dwell in Jerusalem. Both Judaism and Christianity will continue to teach that ultimate Messianic hopes remain anchored in the House of David.

The story of King David—with his later moments of repentance and honor notwithstanding—is an example of *brazen* misuse of power. The term *brazen* is actually too weak to describe the naked power of the pharmaceutical companies considered as responsible for the opioid epidemic. Several high-profile court cases, ongoing prosecutions, and numerous articles and books all reveal the story of the drug OxyContin produced by Purdue Pharma, privately owned by the Sackler families. We are now witnessing an unprecedented public health crisis created by the intentional marketing scheme of a business whose sole goal has been to make billions of dollars regardless of the humans needing pain relief.

Since the drug OxyContin was released in 1996 it has earned $35 billion, addicted millions of people, and is responsible for more than 225,000 overdose deaths [The Center for Disease Control notes 218,000 as of 2017]. Once addicted, it was the drug's high cost that stimulated addicts to find cheaper and more accessible drugs such as heroin and the even more lethal synthetic drugs, like fentanyl. But Purdue Pharma consistently denied all charges: "Our product isn't dangerous—it's *people* who are dangerous."

Ultimately the company admitted that taking OxyContin, even following the company's instructions, will make the patient dependent. But dependence, they argued, is not addiction; hence they would not take responsibility for any abuse of the drug. The company has been penalized as the result of several individual cases and state and federal prosecutions costing the company hundreds of millions of dollars. But to date, none of the individual family members has been held accountable.

Recently, museums that have previously accepted significant gifts from the Sackler families are facing pressure from the public to remove the family name from their buildings. The community must carefully consider the complexity of this multi-generation family and its legacy of philanthropy. Regardless of the amount needed to have your name put on the wing of a museum, there must be an act that most people would agree merits the removal of your name. An act such as the fraudulent marketing of a highly addictive drug sold to people seeking relief from pain.

Yale University removed the name John Calhoun from a residential college because his "legacy as a white supremacist fundamentally conflicts with Yale's mission and values."[2] Yale's mission and values now require a reconsideration of those who donated the Raymond and Beverly Sackler Institute for Biological, Physical and Engineering Sciences, and the Richard Sackler and Jonathan Sackler Professorship of Internal Medicine. You cannot amass a thirteen-billion-dollar family estate, privately own a company still being prosecuted for brazenly cheating both doctors and patients, and then be surprised that there must be some accountability.

Yale, Harvard, Colombia, Oxford, the Guggenheim, the Metropolitan Art Museum, Sackler Gallery in Washington, Louvre, and the Tate Gallery are all now trying to measure whether the Sackler name is worse than "worthless." King David, the greatest King in the Hebrew Bible, behaved as if there were no boundaries for which he was accountable. Nathan then brought the judgement of God. Though David finally acknowledged his transgressions and attempted to sincerely repent, he still was not permitted to build the Temple for God. David learned what all great people must finally learn—you cannot have it all!

We are in a period when the abuse of power by the elite has elicited public rage. We cannot ignore the recriminations of the past nor dismiss the newly empowered voices of victims who are asking the public to punish perpetrators. We don't yet agree about how to respond to those who repent and seek to regain their professional stature. There does seem to be a consensus that past perpetrators of violent racism and hatred ought to be disqualified from both present or future recognition—John Calhoun at Yale is just one example, but institutions across the US are reexamining the legacy of those who are named on buildings and enshrined in statues. It seems logical that we should also recognize when business or political abuse creates an expulsion from public

2. Remnick, "Yale Will Drop John Calhoun's Name," *New York Times*.

acceptance. Purdue Pharma is a fascinating example of naked power, and there is not yet any communal public accountability nor any contrition. Their wealth and philanthropy has created a global legacy that is tragically rooted in a brazen affair of greed and death. We must struggle with both realities, a family name that has been celebrated and is now criminalized.

2 Samuel 11-12 is a narrative text that defies my understanding of biblical intentions. The text provides an explanation for David's relationship with Bathsheba and Solomon's birth. The rest of the text is a damning illumination of the Hebrew Bible's most celebrated King, poet, and the anchor of the ultimate dynasty. Including the full text with all of its murderous vulgarity is one of the Bible's most profound lessons. It is difficult to imagine the generation that edited the final biblical texts, deciding that David's legacy must include the full Bathsheba story, in order to illuminate his humanity as much as his legend. The biblical text guides its human readers to find themselves among the text's developed characters.

Our times now require us to struggle with the complexity of great gifts given from humans whose behavior is sometimes totally unacceptable. The Bible requires that we see the David who is more than a King or a "Star," even as museums and universities argue about the meaning of the Sackler family name. Tufts University is the first to announce the removal of the Sackler name from its school of medicine. "Our students find it objectionable to walk into a building that says Sackler on it when they come in here to get their medical education . . . since the name has become synonymous with the opioid epidemic."[3] We are all missing more than we can admit.

---

3. Barry, "Tufts Removes Sackler," *New York Times*.

8

Esther: Being Afraid
of Fear Itself

A plastic bullet shield that fits into a backpack has become an unexpected but valued gift for a fourteen-year-old about to begin high school. Because we have not yet decided to enact gun control measures that would prevent school shootings in America. There are far too many examples of what frightens us today: the fragility of health care coverage, the opioid epidemic, the negative environment of political extremes, the inability to prevent new acts of global terror, and the global immigration crisis of sixty-eight million people.

"This great Nation will endure as it has endured, will revive and will prosper. So, first of all, let me assert my firm belief that the only thing we have to fear is fear itself—nameless, unreasoning, unjustified terror which paralyzes needed efforts to convert retreat into advance."[1] More than eighty-five years ago, Franklin D. Roosevelt, himself physically paralyzed, spoke to the nation for the first time as its President. In 1933, he challenged the America still stunned and frightened by the Great Depression to use their fear to become stronger and overcome their weakness.

The biblical world faced a period of significant transition twice, 586 BCE and 70 CE, when God's people experienced the destruction of the Temple in Jerusalem and the resulting Exile. "By the rivers of Babylon, there we sat and wept . . . for our captors asked us there for

1. Rosenman, ed., *Public Papers of Franklin D. Roosevelt*, 11–16.

songs, our tormentors, for amusement" (Psalm 137). The Israelites experienced fear and difficulty during the diaspora, the dispersion of the people living outside the biblical land.

The book of Esther—called a *Megillah* or Scroll—is an important example of a biblical text responding to this kind of transition. Most scholars argue that it was written 400-300 BCE, drawing upon Persian and Hellenistic styles. The narrative takes places outside of the biblical land and its issues relate most profoundly for Jews living in the Diaspora, the dispersion following the destruction of the second Temple by Rome in 70 CE. Esther is read only once a year on the festival of Purim. *Megillat* Esther is one of the Five Scrolls[2] and included in the final section of the Hebrew Bible, known as the Writings. Esther is one of only two books in which God does not appear.

The book of Esther begins with a ruler who abuses the power of his position. King Ahasuerus had a royal banquet, during which ". . . the rule for drinking was 'No restrictions.' At the end of the seventh day, the King ordered that Queen Vashti be brought 'wearing her diadem.'" The rabbinic commentators suggest that the King meant she should wear only her crown! She refuses, trying to save her honor, resisting his abuse. Vashti is executed, which provides Esther—an orphan in Shushan—an opportunity to become part of the harem and eventually Ahasuerus' Queen.

The King's abuse is only a hint of the real narrative of fear in the book. Haman, the King's advisor, spends most of the text wanting to exterminate all the Jews! The text signifies that he is an "Agagite"—linked directly to Amalek, Exod 17:8-16, the leader of the warrior people who attacked Israel in the wilderness as they fled Egypt. Amalek is the biblical eternal enemy of all Israelites whose descendants like Haman always hate Jews. Esther will eventually save everyone except Haman and his family who will be killed in acts of brutal revenge by the Jews of Shushan. We read Esther once a year to be reminded of the abuse of shameless power

---

2. The capitalized term, Five Scrolls, literally refers to the Hebrew idiom of the *Chamesh Megilot*. These five different books of the Hebrew Bible are read on five different festivals and always referred to as a group.

and the need to always be aware of the marginalized identity of the Jewish community, especially in the Diaspora. The narrative has a continual thread of fear.

Fear is a common, even essential, element of history, politics, literature, and even religious narratives. Science has taught us that fear triggers an important enzyme in our body, cortisol, the "flight or fight" stimulant. Fear can chemically motivate our body with greater strength, but the same stimulant can hurt our hearts with increased plaque in our arteries. When we are afraid, we can actually do more, but the effects might also be very harmful.

Rather than being afraid of the drunken King's behavior, Esther uses Vashti's demise as her opportunity to become integrated into the royal harem. Mordecai, her uncle, instructs her to keep her identity "masked" fearing that she would face danger if anyone knew she was a Jew, so she tells no one. Eventually she goes through the selection process and the King chooses her to be the Queen. Soon after, Mordecai overhears two terrorists plotting to assassinate the King, which he reports to the now-Queen, Esther. The two would-be killers are captured and executed, evidence of the violence and fear within the royal court.

Mordecai refuses to bow down to Haman, who uses the insult to trigger his desire to destroy *all* Jews. He warns the King using antisemitic propaganda: "There is a certain people, scattered and dispersed among the other peoples in all the provinces of your realm, whose laws are different from those of any other people and who do not obey the King's laws; and it is not in Your Majesty's interest to tolerate them" (Esth 3:8). In other words, the Jews are *so different*, we should be afraid of them, *so let's get rid of those whom we fear!*

This single biblical verse stigmatizes an already marginalized minority, the Jews, and uses fear as the excuse to destroy Jewish life. The King, led astray by Haman's twisted logic, issues a royal order to exterminate all of these unnamed but terrifying people and give all of their wealth and property to Haman. The biblical text emphasizes the fear expressed when the chapter concludes, ". . . but the city of Shushan was dumfounded."

Mordecai now challenges Queen Esther to express herself as a Jew to save her community from Haman: "Do not imagine that you, of all the Jews, will escape with your life by being in the King's palace. On the contrary, if you keep silent in this crisis, relief and deliverance will come to the Jews from another quarter, while you and your father's house will perish!" (Esth 4:13–14) When she became the Queen, she had to hide her identity, but now she must expose herself in order to save her community and her family!

The next four chapters are a biblical thriller. Mordecai and Esther are working to save the Jewish people, Esther decides to use her relationship with the King to expose Haman's plot to destroy her community. She finally admits to the King, "For we have been sold, my people and I, to be destroyed, massacred, and exterminated. The King asked, 'Where is he who dared to order to do this?'" (Esth 7:4–5). Haman and his sons are impaled on the same fifty-cubit stake created to execute Mordecai. The King now reverses all of his previous orders and gives the Jews power over all those who would have harmed them, they now "fear the Jews [*Ye'hudim*] . . ."

Fear motivates a group to survive even as another group feels threatened. During my fourteen years as a full-time academic at St. Cloud State University, I had both the physical and emotional experience of fear stimulating me to find new resources. I remember how exhausted I was from the over-stimulation of being afraid and refusing to consider the consequences of my attempts at being fearless.

The first five years of my position, the university was under the supervision of a federal magistrate. The court wanted to make sure all of the stipulations of the class-action settlement, Zamora v. State of Minnesota, Civ. No. 01-1905, were fully implemented. The university had been accused of antisemitic discrimination. My academic position was created as part of the settlement and one of those stipulations required that there be a full university educational program on antisemitism. I did all I could to convince the administration that shaming the faculty and staff with a required program about their behavior would increase not decrease any animosity to Jews on campus and in the community. I was required to meet with the federal magistrate to explain why I had not implemented the court's order.

I knew the judge from my time as the Senior Rabbi of Temple Israel, so I felt I could be rabbinic in my tone and explanation. I was even sarcastic and asked if the court expected me to make sure the most antisemitic people should sit in the front row so I could tell when they changed their minds. The judge quietly told me that he had always appreciated my teaching and pastoral skills in the sanctuary of Temple Israel, but now I was in his sanctuary and he expected the same respect from me. I was ordered to ensure that all staff and faculty of St. Cloud State University would attend a mandatory ninety-minute educational program on anti-Semitism within thirty days.

My fear that some people would be stigmatized and shamed by the experience was confirmed several times during my tenure. Several people reminded me of the day when "the Jews" made sure everyone knew that we were afraid of being disliked so we got the court to support us. The class action lawsuit was based on employment discrimination, but an environment of prejudice existed on campus as well. Serious discriminatory behavior deeply impacted the few Jews on campus. The campus is in a rural area which was initially populated by German immigrant farmers. Small towns with a Catholic church and a Lutheran church and, depending on your family, there is a church you have never entered. Most of my students had never met a Jew and certainly not a rabbi-professor, and many faculty members expressed their personal frustration about my "special" faculty appointment.

The group that consistently challenged me and then threatened me as a Jew were the social activists who created the anti-racism programs on campus. This faculty group had created a curriculum of several courses dealing with racism in America and had gotten the university to require all students to take one of these courses as a graduation requirement. I first encountered some of them in a meeting for faculty leaders dealing with human rights. I explained my background, my role on campus, and my role in the community. I supported their goal of increasing the scope of diversity courses, but I was opposed to their confrontational style. The group leaders explained that regardless of my background or faculty role, I was a white privileged male and expected to follow their anti-racist ideology.

The majority of white students at St. Cloud State University come from rural Minnesota where there are very few if any persons of color. Many of these students found it difficult to understand that merely being white and privileged also meant being racist. From my experience, the importance of a shared communal recognition of racism was diminished by the more strident charges that simply being white was proof of your racism.

My most serious conflicts with these activists came when I attempted to create a course on antisemitism in America as an addition to the anti-racism courses. In my view, this course met all the Liberal Education requirements for diversity which had been limited to only the anti-racism curriculum. It took four years but finally Jewish Studies 180 was accepted by the committees and the faculty senate as a course that met all the same requirements as any anti-racism course. Though everyone in the administration was sympathetic behind closed doors, no one supported me publicly because of how difficult it was to oppose the anti-racist faculty activists.

I was on campus the week following the horrific mass murder in a Pittsburgh synagogue in 2019, the worst act of antisemitism in American history. I asked the students why they had chosen to take the course, to which the majority answered that it fulfilled the diversity graduation requirement. While this was true, they were taking a course on antisemitism in America while eleven Jews were shot while praying in their own synagogue. This single act of mass murder of Jews changes what it means to study antisemitism. You are not reading about the past but living in America today!

Communities of color are fearful about the persistence of racism on the campus and in the community of St. Cloud, Minnesota. There are six thousand Somali refugees living in St. Cloud who regularly experience a painful combination of racism and Islamophobia. It is one of the tragic ironies of my academic career that a federal court required me to teach the faculty and staff about antisemitism, but I spent most of my actual teaching career in conflict with other faculty who rejected antisemitism as a credible element of anti-racism work. I was afraid of their animosity and I resented that as a Jew who was alone, I had to defend myself and the validity of the antisemitism that brought me to campus.

The biblical authors of Esther were survivors of an ancient Persian "pogrom." Their story inverts the fear of being a Jew living in the ancient Diaspora and creates a festival that has no religious significance. Maybe the first-century rabbis used Esther and Mordecai as heroic models to offset their fear of Rome's destruction of Jerusalem. We cannot reconstruct the context from within which Esther was developed, nor can we access the conversations among those involved in choosing Esther to be included in the Hebrew Bible; all we have is this text.

A seamless bond exists between the text of Esther and the observance of Purim—a festival observed by Jews which is not commanded in the Torah. Let us consider why the rabbis might have added Purim to the calendar. The three pilgrimage festivals, *Pesach* (Passover), *Shavuot* (Pentecost), and *Sukkot* (Tabernacles), are all commanded in the Torah as is the cycle of *Rosh HaShanah* and *Yom Kippur*. But there is a significant time-gap between the end of *Sukkot* in the fall and the beginning of spring when *Pesach* is observed.

The first-century sages were conscious that the diaspora[3] Jewish community had to create a new Judaism without a Temple, priests, and sacrifices. This meant those now called "Jews" would only observe the biblically commanded festivals/holy-days and the weekly Sabbath. They might have feared that more than six months without any festival gatherings—with no reason to gather as a community to observe Jewish rituals—would be difficult for the Jews living in diaspora.

3. Here we are using the word diaspora as an adjective about the community. Other places it is used as Diaspora, the specific period of time, beginning with 70 CE, the destruction of the Second Temple, and ending with the State of Israel in 1948.

The absence of any meaningful calendar observance might have motivated these first-generation rabbis. They used a popular diaspora story to create a non-Torah commanded festival which reminded Jews, just before *Pesach*, of God's salvation of the Israelite slaves. This is a minor festival. A Jewish Queen tells her fellow diaspora Jews about a threat to their identity that could not be solved by God taking them out of Shushan. Diaspora Jews are now responsible for their own safety, and the Scroll of Esther provides them with a fantasy they could become so powerful that their enemies would be afraid. But as textual propaganda, Esther is limited to a single annual reading during the festival of Purim. Esther is a "Queen for a Day,"[4] and though it is only once a year, it is forever!

The rabbis always recognized the link between Haman and Amalek and developed *Shabbat Zachor*. The Sabbath prior to Purim would be used to *Zachor*—remember with an additional portion of Torah to be read: "Remember what Amalek did to you on your journey, after you left Egypt—how, undeterred by the fear of God he surprised you on the march, when you were famished and weary, and cut down all the stragglers in your rear. Therefore, when the Lord your God grants you safety from all your enemies around you, in the land that the Lord your God is giving you as a hereditary portion, you shall blot out the memory of Amalek from under heaven. Do not forget!" (Deut 25:17–19).

The calendar integrates both *Shabbat Zachor* and reading the Scroll of Esther during the festival of Purim to annually remind Jews that the darkest ancient fear of the Israelites has become the necessity of memory, an anchor of Jewish identity. For the rabbis, the historical experience of enemies is a warning about commitment. One contemporary thinker asserts that Jewish tradition demands the burden of an eternal curse. Paradoxically, we have been caught between a past that celebrates victimhood converted

4. This was a radio and then television show (1945–57) which used the tragic circumstances of women's lives as a means of choosing a "Queen for a Day." On the television show the audience listened to three contestants and then applauded for the one they wanted to be a Queen. I have always thought that the woman who becomes Queen Esther is chosen through a series of tragic events, hence the reference to an old reality show.

to revenge. Yet, we must be vigilant about every enemy, past, present, and future. This twisted commitment to "fear of the past" becomes an unspeakable obsession about every unknown enemy of the future!

When Purim is celebrated in the synagogue and Esther is read, everyone present is required when Haman's name is read to make noise to blot out his name. One of the strongest Jewish curses is "*Y'macht Sh'mo!*" ("May his name be blotted out!") which is linked to the commandment regarding Amalek—"blot out his memory." This is that strange paradox, to eternally keep a name for the sole purpose of cursing it and blotting it out! But the practice serves to motivate Jews, not to be victims, but to confront their fears with their own power. The rabbis who ingeniously included the Scroll of Esther and linked Purim to the cursed memory of Amalek, were rightfully fearful of the threats that would challenge the identity of diaspora Jews. And so, they created a ritual by which Jews could stand bravely against those challenges and fears.

We do not need to be reminded of Amalek or Haman seventy-five years after Hitler and Stalin. We have experienced mass murders in a synagogue during Shabbat services in Pittsburgh and Poway, a mosque during services in Christchurch, New Zealand, and three churches during Easter services in Sri Lanka. Jews, Muslims, and Christians murdered while praying in their sanctuaries, all by hateful people of opposing faiths certain that their hatred was justified. We have experienced more than twenty years of mass shootings in schools all over America without any significant legislation. Parents who buried their murdered children have committed suicide because their lives no longer make sense in the face of fear and needless deaths.

There are 68 million refugees around the world as of this writing. These are people who are all afraid of living in their countries of origin, because of war, gang violence, famine, poverty, and the unremitting fear that life has lost all hope. People have died with their children as they tried to find any place to stop and reconstruct any kind of life. Europe has been deeply polarized by refugees from Africa and the Middle East, so that there is a new wave of nationalism fed by the fear of these terrified refugees.

India's ruling Hindu party is emphasizing the fear of Muslim extremists linked to Pakistan in the same way European nationalists agitate the fear of Muslim terrorists. The United States, a country founded by religious refugees from England, the Puritans, are now deeply divided about immigrants and asylum seekers from Central and South America. Thousands of Venezuelans are fleeing for lack of water and food and fear of the army repressing all opposition. Hatred of the other is the easiest product of fear during the chaos of wars, famine, violence, and unchecked terror.

Fear is a human instinct of survival. No one country can save nor help all the people in need. No one leader can resolve all the many global issues that continue to provoke the crisis of mass migration. We cannot be exempt from humans needing help when fear of violence or death overtakes them. We cannot allow the complexity of these millions of terrified humans to be used as political propaganda and the recipe for more government-sanctioned bigotry. Fear draws victims together as a means of survival.

Fear also divides communities by pitting us against one another. We must find the resources to stop the use of fear to fuel hatred. We must engage each other with the shared commitment to be human, especially when others want to use our fear to deny the humanity of others. On Jan. 6, 1941, President Franklin Roosevelt spoke again about fear, and that he hoped for a future that would include the "freedom from fear."

Our current reality is surely not Roosevelt's aspired future. A recent study concluded that nearly 60 percent of high school youth are afraid of a mass school shooting. We must collectively help each other resist the tidal waves of fear. We must create communal resources for our youth to learn how to refashion their fear into resilience. We must reject every effort to divide communities with fear-based bigotry with engaged concerns about the responsibility of being human. Fear is surely an essential characteristic of all humans, but we cannot permit fear to be used to deny anyone's common humanity. Instead, we ought to learn from Esther, who understood that no one can be silent if even a part of the community is threatened. Ultimately our common humanity cannot be ignored.

9

What Are We All *Still* Missing?

We are all, even the best of the best among us, missing "something." This is the essential truth of human nature, and it's confirmed by our reflections on our six biblical role models: Abraham, Rachel, Miriam, Moses, David, and Esther. The concepts raised by engaging these biblical texts are profound and the links with our immediate experiences make the ideas even more complex. To conclude our engagement with these six figures, I have identified four transformative challenges we cannot ignore in our search for what's missing:

- We are all *incomplete, unfinished,* and *imperfect* yet dynamically human.

- *Uncertainty* and *complexity* should be embraced rather than rejected or ignored.

- Our survival depends on our engagement with *community* and *pluralism.*

- We must acknowledge when we have *enough* or have done *enough* and stop our self-destructive striving for more.

Incomplete–Unfinished–Imperfect

Abraham and Rachel, Moses and Miriam, and David and Esther are not *flawed,* but imperfect. We now think of the word *perfect* as meaning without any faults or defects. But the word originally meant to "complete with all the desirable qualities, as good as it is possible to be." Our use of the word perfect to mean without defect is misleading and even dangerous. We use it too frequently without regard to the shadow it casts.

In July 1976, a fourteen-year-old Romanian, Nadia Comaneci, received the first "perfect ten" in Olympic history (in fact, she went on to receive seven additional perfect ten scores during those Olympic games). In the previous eighty years, the organizing institution believed that perfection was not possible, but in 1976 one small Romanian athlete changed everyone's perception. Now everyone knew that a "*perfect ten*" could be achieved.

Today, entire industries sell the guarantee of achieving perfection in education, athletics, arts, or business. People strive for the tens or 100s that will surely open doors to happiness and success, except for many anything less than perfect is simply failure. Life's struggles are too easily expressed in competitive terms, where anything less than "winning" is only losing.

Tests and the resulting grades are educational tools to measure learning; they are not competitions that judge a person's excellence or inferiority. Games of every kind, team sports, individual and even multi-person board or video games are meant to be forms of entertainment. Professional sports have ceased creating opportunities for relaxation, entertainment, and communal spectatorship, and have instead become avenues for billions of gambling dollars and violent community fans. We've placed too much focus on winning, and not enough on sharing time with family and friends.

The dark divisions among us are sustained by these competitions. The scarcity of "winning" jobs, neighborhoods, schools, even vacations require us to compete constantly. We become tragically obsessed with how to validate even a limited number of "perfect" opportunities. We are required to constantly strive for the best, so that we too will be deemed perfect. It is all a scam that disappoints, enrages, and marginalizes the losers. The winners are no less complete or finished, whatever "perfection" they achieve is only in comparison to the losers.

Life's experiences don't offer perfection. There are no perfect jobs, homes, marriages, children, partners, candidates, nor anything else for which we strive. The six biblical figures represent a profound rejection of the "perfect ten." Being human means being profoundly imperfect, incomplete, and unfinished. When we remember that to be perfect simply means to be complete, we realize that "perfection" comes only when our life is finished. But death is surely not the goal for which anyone strives. Furthermore, if we use perfect as a verb, rather than an adjective or adverb, we can altogether remove that imagined goal of being faultless or flawless. As we work to perfect various aspects of our lives, we are on a journey of growth.

A profound lesson about the value of imperfection is offered in the biblical text of Exod 3:14, when God reveals God's name at the Burning Bush: "*Ehyeh-Asher-Ehyeh.*" This is the first and only time in the biblical text that God's Mysterious Divine Name is described. And the words are impossible to translate precisely.

In ancient Hebrew, this phrase is conjugated in the "imperfect" tense, what we call the future, because it is incomplete or unfinished. The "perfect" tense is complete or finished and is understood as the past. The word, *Ehyeh* is the first-person imperfect of the verb "to be." In biblical Hebrew "to be" is only conjugated in the imperfect and perfect tenses but never the present tense. In other words, the classic English translation: "I am that I am" is a complete mistranslation, because the *imperfect* of "to be" is: "I will be."

Moses experiences God as *Ehyeh* because the destiny of this people is still incomplete. These slaves have yet to establish a relationship with God. At the Burning Bush Moses is given the sign of a unique name that can only be heard in the imperfect tense. The text teaches that God can only be understood in the "always-not-yet-completed" mystery of being. *Ehyeh-Asher-Ehyeh* emphasizes the inscrutability of the ancient experience. ". . . [t]he God of the Torah is too shrouded in mystery to be captured by a single insight or point of view. The obvious conclusion is that God does not fit neatly into any one category or mode of experience that we can devise."[1]

1. Seeskin, *Thinking about the Torah*, 82.

Our inability to translate or pronounce the ancient Hebrew name for God is an enduring lesson. God's *untranslatable* ancient name reminds us again and again of how limited we are as humans; we have to create words to describe the Mystery because we cannot even name it. We are humans, inherently *"imperfect,"* which is the only way we can experience God. If we are serious about a search for God in our lives, then we must begin by embracing our true human nature, as unfinished and incomplete.

Uncertainty–Complexity–*Teyku*

Science now stipulates with certainty that there is a complex uncertainty which is determining our universe. This year we learned definitively that our universe is 13.8 billion years old—a construct of time beyond human imagination. Such new vistas of science affirm the uncertainty and complexity of our times. The sheer volume of raw data available to us, and the power of tools like algorithms, seem to suggest that science and technology can determine "certainty."

We are willing to accept assertions far beyond our understanding as scientific certainty. For instance, the "image" of the Black Hole that amazed a global community in early 2019 was accepted without any of us really understanding it. These were not photos, but the data received by radio telescopes sent to computers. The data were transformed into pixels which created an image of an event from 55 million years ago. Consider the utter complexity conveyed by these sentences! We convey information about concepts that are so original that we cannot possibly grasp their meaning.

We need to acknowledge that the scope of the information we are being asked to understand is beyond us. We must have the courage to admit to each other that we are being challenged beyond our capacities. Marco Annunziata, a global economist and business analyst, argues that our current challenges with complexity have put "our cognition itself . . . under attack."[2] He argues that our decision making and our ability to understand are limited resources that cannot manage either the amount or complexity demanded of us. We must collectively admit we are dangerously beyond our human limits.

Our denial or refusal has permitted complexity, uncertainty, and ambiguity to become our norms. Our conflicts over terms like *true, truth, real,* and *fact* illuminate this perfectly. The concept of "post-truth" has been confirmed as a serious and valid category of discourse. The way we define words like "real" and "reality" suggests that we have conceded any factual understanding. "Reality" television is obviously scripted, which means there is no spontaneous "reality." This distorted use of "reality" has become the default meaning. We have not resisted, nor have we rejected, the twisted vocabulary that totally misrepresents the actual complex ambiguity of our lives.

The life struggles that define being human today include uncertainties like economic disparities, the enormity of data, the fragility of security, and the internet's packaging of "truth." Today, the manipulation of these uncertainties intensifies the attraction of certainty. Paradoxically, uncertainty and ambiguity provide us with opportunities to challenge and reject the charisma of "certainty." Uncertainty is a potent stimulant for reflection and critical questions.

Our six biblical figures faced radical change, fear, and historical complexity. In biblical texts, these imagined humans were always challenged by uncertainties like famine, slavery, war, and family disputes. Yet, no matter the challenge, the biblical narratives asserted that none of them become anxious with uncertainty. Surely for the biblical authors it was essential to portray their "faith" as their relationship with a support that can always be trusted: God. There is a significant difference with the more complex and ambiguous reality of actually being human in the twenty-first century. For many, they have lost or chosen to give up any biblical certainty in the face of the past century of genocide, global war,

2. Annunziata and McManus, "The Great Cognitive Depression," *Forbes*.

and the failed competitions of political ideologies. We read about the biblical characters and acknowledge that our struggles require a very different recognition of uncertainty.

The rabbis were aware that uncertainty and complexity signified important characteristics of human limits. These limits were confirmed when the rabbinic sages taught that some issues "stand forever in the state of insolubility—the issues remain unsolved!" Some have interpreted the idiom, *"teyku"* to mean that all unsolved problems and unanswered questions will be left until Elijah the prophet comes to announce the Messianic age or waiting forever. Like the scientists who now insist that there is a not-yet-discovered factor which will correct our miscalculations, the Talmudic sages were ready to permit hundreds of legal questions to be answered only when the answers were no longer relevant. In other words, there is profound ancient wisdom in acknowledging that some questions will always remain beyond our minds—that uncertainty and complexity will outlast our false presumptions.

The indescribable reality of being human today cannot be fit into the simple patterns of earlier times and ideas. The amount of change we experience requires profound risks without guarantees of sustaining of comfort. We are being asked to accept new concepts before we fully understand what the change means. Our ability to adapt requires that we learn new skills and accept different values, especially about being part of a greater community of individuals.

Community–Pluralism

Abraham, Rachel, Moses, Miriam, David, and Esther are animated by biblical texts that link their lives to community. Abraham initiates a community of immigrants from ancient Iraq who claim their identity with the One God. Rachel is the last matriarch of these nomadic shepherds, a clan who moves to Egypt to survive a famine and become a people. Moses and Miriam's identities are totally interwoven with the enslaved and then freed Israelites, who experience redemption and revelation but cannot claim their

destiny. Both King David and Queen Esther are defined by responsibilities to the communities they rule, but their legacies link Jewish communities far beyond their times and texts.

The Exodus—redemption from slavery—is the story of a
community. The revelation of Torah at Sinai is done in the desert for the entire community. The Golden Rule (Lev 19:18) is the
universal ethical teaching, "love your neighbor as yourself," which
assumes the relationship of a "neighbor" as the standard. The text
also includes prophetic judgements about social indifference to
the poor and isolated. It is always the community's responsibility
to care for the hungry, naked, and homeless.

We experience learning in a community—the school—where
acquiring social skills is just as important as mastering concepts.
Our very first learned task of sharing cannot be learned as an individual, but only in relationships, ideally in a group. We learn the
most important aspects of ourselves from our engagement with
others, not as individuals. At a time when loneliness and solitary
depression are serious problems, when social media platforms
have technologically replaced relationships and community, we
must strive to return to the communal experience.

The Hebrew Bible teaches the inherent pluralism within a
clan of nomads that becomes a community of slaves and then a
freed community searching for its destiny. The Torah describes
the ideally inclusive community, "You stand here today, all of you
. . . your tribal heads, your elders and officials, all the men of Israel, your children, your wives, even the stranger within your camp,
from the woodchopper to water drawer . . ." (Deut 29:9–10). This
conveys the ancient social totality of the whole, all sharing in an
experience of commitment, individuals willing to be linked beyond the limits of self.

We must renew a commitment to the value of a pluralist
community rather than the constant celebration of individuals
and competing identities. The Hebrew Bible never commands
the tolerance or diversity that is the minimum now required by
institutions and legal definitions. We are bitterly divided, and
our legal system is now in charge of our ethical standards. From

the most profound realization of the legalizing of marriage of all persons regardless of gender or orientation, to the shameful individual rights campaign of bakers who fight for their right to refuse someone a cake! These realities remind us of how meaningless the value of tolerance has become.

Tolerance is the lowest possible rank of begrudging acceptance. The verb "to tolerate" expresses an acceptance which can only be rude silence, "I can tolerate this, but must I?" Diversity has also lost much of its meaning in our political discourse, and rarely helps us understand the dynamic pluralism of a community, except as it labels its embattled individual political identities.

The pluralism for which I continue to strive is difficult, messy, confusing, and still a far-off goal on the social horizon of most people. Pluralism means that we do not define ourselves by rejecting Others. Jews should not explain themselves as "not believing that Jesus is the Messiah." We should never define ourselves based on who we reject. I understand God as being radically universal, One Single Divine presence for all the many religious communities. There is not a Jewish God, Christian God (Catholic and Protestant), Muslim God, Hindu God, Buddhist God, and God of the many indigenous peoples. There is simply and only One God. We have historically rejected the gods, idols, stories, beliefs, rituals, and identity of those who differ from us, and used *our* rejection as our starting point.

The pattern of identifying as *not* being (i.e., blank) has been copied into nationalities, politics, and economics. Pluralism begins with the assumption of a plurality of truths that are defined by time, place, and even the simple experience of chance. When we are naturally able and willing to accept more than a single truth, we will not let our social, cultural, and historical realities challenge and limit our opportunities. Pluralism requires more effort, but the eventual celebration of actual diversity makes our lives dynamic.

We are living at a time when the social differences of race, gender, and sexual orientation are no longer the barriers that limited so many. But the legislative and judicial paths of equality still require complete social integration of real pluralism. The reaction to this complete social transformation as well as demographic shifts has been painful rage. Pluralism demands that the community embrace and celebrate its complex potential rather than accept its new reality as a victim of polarized politics.

Enough–Perspective

Often the time and effort spent in our search for what we are missing distorts our sense that what we've finally found is never "enough." Our hopes and expectations are always greater than what we find, or we have, or we need! "Enough" is one of the old simple words that is used so often and so much that we long ago lost our critical understanding.

An adequate or sufficient or required or acceptable or satisfactory amount of everything. Surely there is nothing more basic to human nature as our inability to determine when we've actually got enough: enough food, enough love, enough clothes, enough money, enough happiness, and enough success. There is no way to instinctively know when you have "enough" of what you need or want. The old truism, "Don't go shopping when you are hungry," teaches us that our hunger, not our actual need, will distort what we imagine to be enough.

Today technology constantly offers and promises us *more*! The consumer is invited to shop on a seemingly infinite platform of ever-present stores that encourage *more* (even while promising that the prices will be *less*!). For me eating from a buffet table is difficult because it requires an internalized awareness of what is truly enough. We all want more—that's human nature. But we don't always need more. I tried to explain to my children that I would always provide them with what they needed, but not always with what they wanted. It is our challenge to find the limit of what is truly enough.

The idea of "enough" as a limit is experienced when we use the word as a command to stop—Enough! The power of our single word conveys the speaker's full commitment that whatever was happening must end immediately. This expression carries a tone of serious, even angry, certainty, there are no questions or discussions permitted—I said enough! In Brazilian Portuguese the idiom is "*Chega!*" or "it has arrived!" We are at the end—*enough.*

We use the word in both contexts and rarely ask ourselves why the same word can mean both a vague undetermined amount and an urgent and totally committed conclusion. Our experience of the word and the breadth of its meanings helps us to discern the depth of our own sense of enough from which we must learn *perspective.* How far away should you stand in order to fully "see" a painting, sculpture, or understand an issue? Learning how to "see" something differently is a skill often gained like wisdom, only through the experiences of life itself. I measure the concept of "enough" very differently today at seventy-three than at thirty-seven, and no one could have instructed me how to change my perspective. Being human permits us to grow every day in our experience of our needs, our abilities, and our desires. We have "enough" only when we recognize what all the other concepts really mean.

The Passover service uses a ninth-century poem/song to teach the importance of historical perspective. "*Dayenu*": "It Would Have Been Enough." The song is one of several that has been integrated to remind all those at the table of history—both the details of the events that have happened, and the later conclusions we have made about those events. When the past is compared to the present, we have perspective to understand how far we have come and how much we needed the past to make this progress.

Dayenu (Lyrics in English) (a sample of the verses)

If God had brought us out from Egypt, and had not carried out judgments against them, *Dayenu,* it would have sufficed us!

If God had split the sea for us and had not taken us through it on dry land/*Dayenu,* it would have sufficed us!

If God had taken us through the sea on dry land, and had not drowned our oppressors in it, *Dayenu,* it would have sufficed us!

If God had supplied our needs in the desert for forty years, and had not fed us the manna, *Dayenu,* it would have sufficed us!

If God had given us the Shabbat and had not brought us before Mount Sinai, *Dayenu,* it would have sufficed us!

If God had given us the Torah and had not brought us into the land of Israel, *Dayenu,* it would have sufficed us!

Everyone loves singing the chorus, "*Dayenu,* Die, Die . . . aynu." The song has fifteen verses, so we are all waiting for someone to say with that authoritative certainty: "*Dayenu*"—Enough! The song teaches a profound idea by listing the biblical chronology. Sinai and Torah cannot be appreciated until the people are free and crossed the sea.

In other words, you cannot understand the difference between real need and the frustrations of delayed gratification until you've experienced enough life to offer perspective and wisdom. "Enough" cannot be understood by measuring or asking others; you simply have to experience "too much." Sometimes we misjudge that what we need, our missing piece, is not enough. Our perspective has been distorted in the competition with others or in our striving to be perfect.

These four transformative challenges are positive corrections in our intense, hyper-individualized, destructively competitive times.

- We are all *incomplete, unfinished,* and *imperfect* yet dynamically human.

- *Uncertainty* and *complexity* should be embraced rather than rejected or ignored.

- Our survival depends on our engagement with *community* and *pluralism.*

- We must acknowledge when we have or have done *enough* and stop our self-destructive striving for more.

Each term is already in our vocabulary, but we now must use and integrate their meanings more fully, more consciously. None of us is a passive victim to the challenges of our time; our search for "missing pieces" is a shared journey among all human beings. How we choose to engage our search or deny our sense of being lost or our need for help are the identifying markers that will finally put a name on the finished puzzle.

With the rapid development of AI (artificial intelligence), one must wonder if sometime soon you will be able to ask "Siri" or "Alexa" as you walk out of the door, "What am I missing?" Maybe they will have collected enough data about our behavior to answer correctly, "Your house keys and backpack." Even if or when we can ask questions that can be predicted by an algorithm, some questions will remain unanswerable without engaging with deep personal reflection. Questions like: "Where can I find more resilience or serenity in my life?" Our most enduring values cannot be located through our still growing data banks. If Google can someday answer any question that can be asked, then the most profound questions become meaningless.

This book was inspired by a simple but intentionally open-ended question. Such a question stimulates engagement, provokes more questions, and hopefully creates conversations and communal awareness. The answers produced by technology diminish our yearning to ask deeper questions, and the ease of data retrieval has replaced our need to seek answers. We have become addicted to the speed with which information can be accessed. Students no longer have a reason to go into library "stacks" or even open dictionaries, because their cell phones are mini-computers created to provide answers but not encourage the quest of questions.

I have instructed my students for decades that formulating a good question is much more valuable than a twenty-five-page essay restating other people's answers. Unanswered questions link decades of humans; questions are shared ideas being rethought from new contexts. Listening or reading and then stopping to wonder, and then writing a few words, and then finding the courage to raise your hand, and finally with your heart beating and your eyes looking around for support, you ask your question. You cannot ever measure the growth gained in just those moments.

None of us will ever know if the six biblical characters asked, "What am I missing?" But through them we have been able to ask questions about ourselves. Biblical texts produce amazing questions that defy certainty. Our shared search in these pages is not intended to provide a Power Point to be used for everybody anywhere. If every reader is encouraged, empowered, or even provoked to ask themselves a new question which they shared and thought about, then this project is a success.

As I have gathered my missing pieces and given others their pieces, I have grown more confident because of questions. Questions stimulate engagement. You cannot live with a question as a solitary person; you want to think out loud, you need to discuss, debate, get feedback. The best questions force us to take a position. You cannot remain neutral when you are honestly open yourself to the pluralism of ideas. Life-changing questions are invitations to participation without any promises of immediate happiness. It is the growth from such participation and the shared anticipation of our communal conversations that describe my ideal of being human.

The invitation for your participation has now expired. As the reader, you can move on to more reading and solicit other readers to engage in conversations. You can be daring and formulate your own questions to stimulate your conversations. You can stop and reflect on what you have read and await an undefined time and engage your life differently. You can smile and quietly remember where you left something you were sure was missing!

December 20, 2019
Rio de Janeiro

Bibliography

Ades, Robert. "Winnicott / The 'Good-Enough Mother' Radio Broadcasts." *OUPblog* (January 2016). https://blog.oup.com/2016/12/winnicott-radio-broadcasts/.

"AIDSinfo." UNAIDS. https://aidsinfo.unaids.org/.

Annunziata, Marco, and Mickey McManus. "The Great Cognitive Depression." *Forbes* (January 11, 2019). https://www.forbes.com/sites/marcoannunziata/2019/01/11/the-great-cognitive-depression/#3586cf4474c1.

Barry, Ellen. "Tufts Removes Sackler Name Over Opioids: 'Our Students Find It Objectionable.'" *New York Times* (December 5, 2019). https://www.nytimes.com/2019/12/05/us/tufts-sackler-name-opioids.html.

Ben-Chaim, Moshe. "Why the Temple Could Not Be Built by King David." http://www.mesora.org/DavidsTemple.htm.

Berlin, Adele, and Marc Zvi Breitler. *The Jewish Study Bible.* Oxford: Oxford University Press, 2004.

Bloom, Paul. "The Baby in the Well: The Case Against Empathy." *New Yorker* (May 20, 2013). https://www.newyorker.com/magazine/2013/05/20/the-baby-in-the-well.

Bradatan, Costica. "In Praise of Failure." *New York Times* (December 15, 2013). https://opinionator.blogs.nytimes.com/2013/12/15/in-praise-of-failure/.

Bridges, Tyler. "David Duke Is Back—Or Is He?" *Moment Magazine* (September 7, 2017). https://momentmag.com/opinion-david-duke-back/.

Brody, Jane. "Hooked on Our Smartphones." *New York Times* (January 9, 2017). https://www.nytimes.com/2017/01/09/well/live/hooked-on-our-smartphones.html.

Brooks, Arthur. "Our Culture of Contempt." *New York Times* (March 2, 2019). https://www.nytimes.com/2019/03/02/opinion/sunday/political-polarization.html.

Brooks, Geraldine. *The Secret Chord: A Novel.* New York: Penguin, 2015.

Bruni, Frank. "A 'Disgusting' Yale Professor Moves On." *New York Times* (March 19, 2019). https://www.nytimes.com/2019/03/19/opinion/nicholas-christakis-yale.html.

Buber, Martin. *Moses*. London: East and West Library, 1947.

———. *On the Bible*. Edited by Nathan N. Glazer. Schocken, 1968.

Buber, Martin, and Frank Rozenweig. *Scripture and Translation*. Translated by Lawrence Rosenwald and Everett Fox. Bloomington: Indiana University Press, 1994.

Crosby, Harry. *Transit of Venus: Poems*. Paris: Black Sun, 1931.

David, Ariel. "How the Jews Invented God, and Made Him Great." *Haaretz* (June 16, 2016). https://www.haaretz.com/archaeology/.premium.MAGAZINE-how-the-jews-invented-god-and-made-him-great-1.5392677.

Decuir, Sharlene Sinegal. "Good Riddance to Confederate Monuments." *New York Times* (April 28, 2017). https://www.nytimes.com/2017/04/28/opinion/good-riddance-to-confederate-monuments.html.

Diamond, James. "YHWH: The God That Is vs. the God That Becomes." *The Torah*. https://www.thetorah.com/article/yhwh-the-god-that-is-vs-the-god-that-becomes.

Eisner, Jane. "In Search of a Prophet." *Forward* (October 9, 2018). https://forward.com/opinion/411458/in-search-of-a-prophet/.

Eliot, T. S. "Preface." In *Transit to Venus*, by Harry Crosby. Paris: Black Sun Press, 1931.

Farely, Audrey. "Big Pharma Is Pushing a Big Lie." *The New Republic* (May 10, 2019). https://newrepublic.com/article/153864/innovation-drug-price-myth.

Fausset, Richard. "Tempers Flare Over Removal of Confederate Statues in New Orleans." *New York Times* (May 7, 2017). https://www.nytimes.com/2017/05/07/us/new-orleans-monuments.html.

Feldman, Louis H. *"Remember Amalek!" Vengeance, Zealotry, and Group Destruction in the Bible According to Philo, Pseudo-Philo, and Josephus*. Cincinnati: Hebrew Union College Press, 2004.

Fischer, Agneta. "Contempt: A Hot Feeling Hidden Under a Cold Jacket." *Semantic Scholar* (2011). https://www.semanticscholar.org/paper/Contempt%3A-a-hot-feeling-hidden-under-a-cold-jacket-Fischer/d403c655bbe5b0804fb5c99c396337a5bc29750e.

Fishbane, Michael. *The Exegetical Imagination: On Jewish Thought and Theology*. Cambridge: Harvard University Press, 1998.

———, ed. *The Midrashic Imagination: Jewish Exegesis, Thought and History*. Albany: State University of New York Press, 1993.

Frederick, William C. "The Virtual Reality of Fact vs. Value: A Symposium Commentary." *Business Ethics Quarterly* 4, no. 2 (1994): 171–173.

Friedman, Thomas L. "Dancing in a Hurricane." *New York Times* (November 19, 2016). https://www.nytimes.com/2016/11/20/opinion/sunday/dancing-in-a-hurricane.html.

Gilbert, Martin. *Churchill and the Jews: A Lifelong Friendship*. New York: Henry Holt, 2007.

Goldstone, Brian. "The Pain Refugees: The Forgotten Victims of America's Opioid Crisis." *Harper's* (April 2018). https://harpers.org/archive/2018/04/the-pain-refugees/.

Green, Alexander. "Power, Deception and Comedy: The Politics of Exile in the Book of Esther." Jerusalem Center for Public Affairs (April 12, 2012). http://jcpa.org/article/power-deception-and-comedy-the-politics-of-exile-in-the-book-of-esther-by-alexander-green/.

Guenther, Lisa, and Abigail Levin. "White 'Power' and the Fear of Replacement." *New York Times* (August 28, 2017). https://www.nytimes.com/2017/08/28/opinion/white-power-and-the-fear-of-replacement.html.

Hadari, Atar. "Why the Lord Doesn't Allow David to Build the Temple." *Mosaic* (April 20, 2017). https://mosaicmagazine.com/observation/religion-holidays/2017/04/why-the-lord-doesnt-allow-david-to-build-the-temple/.

Herper, Matthew. "Why Did That Drug Price Increase 6,000%? It's the Law." *Forbes* (February 10, 2017). https://www.forbes.com/sites/matthewherper/2017/02/10/a-6000-price-hike-should-give-drug-companies-a-disgusting-sense-of-deja-vu/#75f3ba7f1f5.

Heschel, Abraham J. *Moral Grandeur and Spiritual Audacity*. Edited by Susannah Heschel. New York: Farrar, Straus and Giroux, 1996.

———. *A Passion for the Truth*. New York: Farrar, Straus and Giroux, 1973.

———. *Who Is Man?* Stanford: Stanford University Press, 1965.

Heuck, Douglas. "Elie Wiesel and the One Indestructible Human Quality." *Pittsburgh Quarterly*, Between the Issues (July 6, 2016). https://pittsburghquarterly.com/between-the-issues/item/1139-elie-wiesel-one-indestructible-human-quality.html.

Huang, Karen, Alison Wood Brooks, Ryan W. Buell, Brian Hall, and Laura Huang. "Mitigating Malicious Envy: Why Successful Individuals Should Reveal Their Failures." *Harvard Business School* (2018). https://www.hbs.edu/faculty/Publication%20Files/18-080_56688b05-34cd-47ef-adeb-aa7050b93452.pdf.

Jacobs, Louis. *Teyku: The Unsolved Problem in the Babylonian Talmud*. London: Leo Baeck College Publication, 1981.

Japhet, Sara. "Survival and Revival: Megillat Esther and Ezra-Nehemiah." *TheTorah*. https://www.thetorah.com/article/survival-and-revival-megillat-esther-and-ezra-nehemiah.

Jeanrond, Werner G., and Jennifer L. Rike. *Radical Pluralism & Truth: David Tracy and the Hermeneutics of Religion*. New York: Crossroad, 1991.

"Jew, v." Oxford English Dictionary Online. https://www.oed.com/.

Jones, Lynne. "Each Scar Is Different: The More We Label Every Trauma with PTSD, the Less It Means." *Aeon* (May 22, 2014). https://aeon.co/essays/the-more-we-label-every-trauma-with-ptsd-the-less-it-means.

Jones, Robert P. "The Rage of White, Christian America." *New York Times* (November 20, 2016). https://www.nytimes.com/2016/11/11/opinion/campaign-stops/the-rage-of-white-christian-america.html.

Kadari, Tamar. "Rachel: Midrash and Aggadah." *Jewish Women's Archives.* https://jwa.org/encyclopedia/article/rachel-midrash-and-aggadah.

Kaminsky, Joel S. "Who Is David?" *Jewish Review of Books* (Fall 2015). https://jewishreviewofbooks.com/articles/1873/who-is-david/.

Kaplan, Rabbi Aryeh, trans. *The Seven Beggars and Other Kabbalistic Tales of Rebbe Nachman of Breslov.* Woodstock: Jewish Lights, 2005.

Kepnes, Steven, ed. *Interpreting Judaism In a Postmodern World.* New York: New York University Press, 1996.

Khazan, Olga. "The Problem with Being Perfect." *Atlantic* (November 5, 2018). https://www.theatlantic.com/health/archive/2018/11/how-perfectionism-can-be-destructive/574837/.

Kirsch, Adam. "Lie to Me: Fiction in the Post-Truth Era." *New York Times* (January 15, 2017). https://www.nytimes.com/2017/01/15/books/lie-to-me-fiction-in-the-post-truth-era.html.

Kirsch, Jonathan. *King David: The Real Life of the Man Who Ruled Israel.* New York: Ballantine, 2000.

Koplow, Michael. "The End of the Jewish People Is Here." *Forward* (June 11, 2018). https://forward.com/opinion/402932/the-end-of-the-jewish-people-is-here/.

Kraft, Dina. "The Power Women of Purim: Bringing Back Vashti and Esther in the #MeToo Era." *Haaretz* (February 26, 2018). https://www.haaretz.com/israel-news/.premium-the-power-women-of-purim-vashti-and-esther-in-the-age-of-metoo-1.5826889.

Kushner, Lawrence. *Honey from the Rock: Visions of Jewish Mystical Renewal.* San Francisco: Harper and Row, 1977.

LaCocque, Andre, and Paul Ricoeur. *Thinking Biblically: Exegetical and Hermeneutical Studies.* Chicago: University of Chicago Press, 1998.

Lalami, Laila. "The Identity Politics of Whiteness." *New York Times* (November 27, 2016). https://www.nytimes.com/2016/11/27/magazine/the-identity-politics-of-whiteness.html.

Leiber, David, ed. *Etz Hayim: Torah and Commentary.* New York: The Rabbinical Assembly and The United Synagogue of Conservative Judaism, 2001.

Levinas, Emmanuel. *Difficult Freedom: Essays on Judaism.* Translated by Sean Hand. Baltimore: Johns Hopkins University Press, 1990.

Livingstone, Josephine. "Who Owns the Crusades?" *New Republic* (June 11, 2019). https://newrepublic.com/article/154170/owns-crusades.

Malone, Noreen. "Algorithm Shame: The Feeling of Being Seen by the Algorithm." *Intelligencer* (October 11, 2018). http://nymag.com/intelligencer/2018/10/algorithm-shame-the-feeling-of-being-seen-by-the-algorithm.html.

Maltz, Judy. "Purim." *Haaretz* (December 13, 2019). http://www.haaretz.com/misc/tags/TAG-purim—1.5599208.

Mangurian, Christina, Eleni Linos, Urmimala Sarkar, Carolyn Rodriguez, and Reshma Jagsi. "What's Holding Women in Medicine Back from Leadership." *Harvard Business Review* (June 19, 2018). https://hbr.org/2018/06/whats-holding-women-in-medicine-back-from-leadership.

McEwen, Bruce. "When Is Stress Good for You?" *Aeon* (July 11, 2017). https://aeon.co/essays/how-stress-works-in-the-human-body-to-make-or-break-us.

McKenzie, Steven L. *King David: A Biography.* Oxford: Oxford University Press, 2002.

Meier, Barry. "Origins of an Epidemic: Purdue Pharma Knew Its Opioids Were Widely Abused." *New York Times* (May 29, 2018). https://www.nytimes.com/2018/05/29/health/purdue-opioids-oxycontin.html.

Meir, Tamar. "Esther: Midrash and Aggadah." *Jewish Women's Archives* (March 20, 2009). https://jwa.org/encyclopedia/article/esther-midrash-and-aggadah.

———. "Miriam: Midrash and Aggadah." *Jewish Women's Archives* (March 20, 2009). https://jwa.org/encyclopedia/article/miriam-midrash-and-aggadah.

"Midrash Rabbah: Bereshit Rabbah 38:13." *Sepharia.* https://www.sefaria.org/Bereishit_Rabbah.38.13?lang=bi.

"Midrash Rabbah: Shemot Rabbah 2:2." *Sepharia.* https://www.sefaria.org/Shemot_Rabbah.2.2?lang=bi.

"Mitch Landrieu's Speech on the Removal of Confederate Monuments in New Orleans." *New York Times* (May 23, 2017). https://www.nytimes.com/2017/05/23/opinion/mitch-landrieus-speech-transcript.html.

Overbye, Dennis. "Darkness Visible, Finally: Astronomers Capture First Ever Image of a Black Hole." *New York Times* (April 10, 2019). https://www.nytimes.com/2019/04/10/science/black-hole-picture.html.

———. "Our Universe's Very Dusty Early, Early Beginnings." *New York Times* (March 8, 2017). https://www.nytimes.com/2017/03/08/science/oldest-dust-in-universe.html.

———. "Third Gravitational Wave Detection, From Black-Hole Merger 3 Billion Light Years Away." *New York Times* (June 1, 2017). https://www.nytimes.com/2017/06/01/science/black-holes-collision-ligo-gravitational-waves.html.

Remnick, Noah. "Yale Will Drop John Calhoun's Name from Building." *The New York Times* (February 11, 2017). https://www.nytimes.com/2017/02/11/us/yale-protests-john-calhoun-grace-murray-hopper.html.

Ricoeur, Paul. *The Conflict of Interpretations: Essays in Hermeneutics.* Edited by Don Ihide. Evanston: Northwestern University Press, 1974.

———. *Essays on Biblical Interpretation.* Edited by Lewis Mudge. Philadelphia: Fortress, 1980.

———. *Figuring the Sacred: Religion, Narrative and Imagination.* Edited by Mark I. Wallace. Minneapolis: Fortress, 1995.

———. *History and Truth.* Translated by Charles A. Kelbey. Evanston: Northwestern University Press, 1965.

———. *Interpretation Theory: Discourse and the Surplus of Meaning.* Dallas: Texas Christian University Press, 1976.

———. *The Just.* Translated by David Pellauer. Chicago: University of Chicago Press, 2000.

———. *Memory, History, Forgetting.* Translated by Kathleen Blamey and David Pellauer. Chicago: University of Chicago Press, 2004.

———. *Oneself as Another.* Translated by Kathleen Blamey. Chicago: University of Chicago Press, 1990.

Rizzo, Albert A., and Maria T. Schultheis. "Expanding the Boundaries of Psychology: The Application of Virtual Reality." *Taylor & Francis, Ltd.* 13, no. 2 (2002): 133–40.

Rosenman, Samuel, ed. *The Public Papers of Franklin D. Roosevelt, Volume Two: The Year of Crisis, 1933.* New York: Random House, 1938.

Rowghani, Ali. "How Do You Measure Leadership?" *YCombinator* (January 19, 2017). https://blog.ycombinator.com/how-do-you-measure-leadership/.

Scherman, Nosson, ed. *The Chumash: The Torah: Haftaros and Megillos with a Commentary Anthologized from the Rabbinic Writings.* Brooklyn: Mesorah Publications, 1993.

Schuster, Ruth. "Mystery of Galactic Hyperspeed Cracked: It's the Universe's Imperfection." *Haaretz* (January 30, 2017). https://www.haaretz.com/science-and-health/mystery-of-galactic-motion-cracked-voids-repel-1.5492267.

Science 37, no. 2 (Special Focus: Media, Religion and Society in Iran) (2009): 208–31.

Seeskin, Kenneth. *Thinking about the Torah: A Philosopher Reads the Bible.* Philadelphia: Jewish Publication Society, 2016.

Serpell, Namwali. "The Banality of Empathy." *NYR Daily | New York Review of Books* (March 2, 2019). https://www.nybooks.com/daily/2019/03/02/the-banality-of-empathy/.

Shaughnessy, Brooke Ann, and Claudia Verena Peus. "When Power Paralyzes: The Role of the Type of Power, Culture, and the Value of Cultural Norms." *Academy of Management Proceedings* 2013, no. 1 (February 23, 2018). https://doi.org/10.5465/ambpp.2013.10739abstract.

Silverstein, Shel. *The Missing Piece.* New York: Harper Collins, 1976.

Smith, Martin, Simon Sherry, Vanja Vidovic, Don Saklofske, Joachim Stober, and Aryn Benoit. "Perfectionism and the Five-Factor Model of Personality: A Meta-Analytic Review." *Personality and Social Psychology Review* 23 (October 21, 2019): 367–90. doi:10.1177/1088868318814973.

Soloveichik, Meir Y. "King David." *First Things* (January 2017). https://www.firstthings.com/article/2017/01/king-david.

Staples, Brent. "Opinion | How the Swastika Became a Confederate Flag." *New York Times* (May 22, 2017). https://www.nytimes.com/2017/05/22/opinion/white-supremacist-confederate-monuments-nazi.html.

Stohr, Karen. "Our New Age of Contempt." *New York Times* (January 23, 2017). https://www.nytimes.com/2017/01/23/opinion/our-new-age-of-contempt.html.

Tisserand, Michael. "In New Orleans, Racism's History Is Harder Than Stone." *New York Times* (May 8, 2017). https://www.nytimes.com/2017/05/08/opinion/in-new-orleans-racisms-history-is-harder-than-stone.html.

Tracy, David. *Dialogue with the Other: Inter-Religious Dialogue.* Grand Rapids: Eerdmans, 1991.

———. *Plurality and Ambiguity: Hermeneutics, Religion and Hope.* San Francisco: Harper and Row, 1987.

Twilley, Nicola. "The Terrifying Lessons of a Pandemic Simulation." *New Yorker* (June 1, 2018). https://www.newyorker.com/science/elements/the-terrifying-lessons-of-a-pandemic-simulation.

Unterman, Yael. "Esther, Heroine for Those Who Must Hide." Blog. *Times of Israel* (March 7, 2017). https://blogs.timesofisrael.com/esther-heroine-for-those-who-must-hide/.

Wolak, Arthur J. *Religion and Contemporary Management: Moses as a Model for Effective Leadership.* London: Anthem, 2016.

Yerushalmi, Yosef Hayim. *Freud's Moses: Judaism Terminable and Interminable.* The Franz Rosenzweig Lecture Series. New Haven: Yale University Press, 1993.

CPSIA information can be obtained
at www.ICGtesting.com
Printed in the USA
FSHW021252010420
68683FS